Other Books by Dr. Les Carter

The Anger Trap

People Pleasers

Christ in You

(with Dr. Frank Minirth)

The Anger Workbook for Christian Parents

The Anger Workbook

The Freedom from Depression Workbook

The Worry Workbook

The Choosing to Forgive Workbook

Grace and Divorce

God's Healing Gift to Those Whose Marriages Fall Short

Dr. Les Carter

JOSSEY-BASS
A Wiley Imprint
www.josseybass.com

Published by Jossey-Bass
A Wiley Imprint
989 Market Street, San Francisco, CA 94103-1741   www.josseybass.com

Scripture taken from the NEW AMERICAN STANDARD BIBLE®, Copyright © 1960, 1962, 1963, 1968, 1971, 1972, 1973, 1975, 1977, 1995 by The Lockman Foundation. Used by permission.

All cases cited in this book are composites of the author's actual cases. Names and specific details have been changed to maintain confidentiality.

Jossey-Bass books and products are available through most bookstores. To contact Jossey-Bass directly call our Customer Care Department within the U.S. at 800-956-7739, outside the U.S. at 317-572-3986, or fax 317-572-4002.

Jossey-Bass also publishes its books in a variety of electronic formats. Some content that appears in print may not be available in electronic books.

Library of Congress Cataloging-in-Publication Data

Carter, Les.
Grace and divorce: God's healing gift to those whose marriages fall short / Les Carter.
    p. cm.
    ISBN 0-7879-7581-8 (alk. paper)
    1. Divorce—Religious aspects—Christianity. 2. Divorced people—Religious life. I. Title.
BT707.C37 2004
248.8'46—dc22   2004011285

Printed in the United States of America
FIRST EDITION
HB Printing   10 9 8 7 6 5 4 3 2 1

Contents

As a youth I witnessed how my dad, Ed Carter,
treated "underdogs" with great respect and goodness.
His living illustrations of grace became the
foundation for much of my adult thinking.
This book is dedicated with
admiration to him.

Acknowledgments

Great thanks are given to Marti Miller and Brian Wade for their assistance in the preparation of this manuscript. Also, Martha Hook has taken a tremendous interest in this project and proven invaluable in her suggestions and efforts to create a clean manuscript.

Introduction

I am often frustrated when I hear people discuss their reactions to someone's divorce. Many people in my circle of acquaintances are, as I am, conservative evangelical Christians who regularly consult the scriptures for guidance regarding life's decisions. As they survey the teachings of the Bible, they see that God has high regard for the marriage vows, going so far to state, "I hate divorce." That must be why some assume they are being disloyal to God if they act too kindly toward individuals who are going through divorce. As a result, some Christians give the cold shoulder when they learn of one going through a divorce, others may not allow their kids to play with one another, and still others feel the need to give unsolicited advice.

The result of this tentative, less-than-friendly response to divorcees is that many decent people feel disenfranchised from the church—from the very ones they need most in a time of personal crisis. My desire in writing this book is to help soften the stigma divorced Christians experience, explaining how Jesus never intended us to be so fixed in our beliefs about right and wrong that we lose the ability to love those who have not met His perfect standards. I have no intention of shrugging off divorce as a simple problem that can be taken lightly. It is serious and should be the remedy only of last resort. I do write, however, with the notion that the best way to respond to people when they are in a down position is through the wonderful gift of grace.

All Christians are stained. We are all imperfect. We differ in the manifestations of our imperfections; nonetheless we each suffer from some form of unrighteousness. God's grace is not dependent on how imperfect we are. If people who have never been divorced can receive grace, so can those who have. There is no seeker of Christ who is more or less in need of His cleansing, since we each have an equal need for His healing power.

My main purpose in this book is to encourage consistency regarding the subject of grace and to show that people who have fallen short of God's perfect principles are positioned to receive healing words, and we do not want to miss such an opportunity to be a conduit for healing. Like Jesus, we can be true to God's standards for righteous living even as we minister to one another amid great need.

The words written here are the result of prayer and much contemplation after years of counseling and being involved in the lives of people who are hurting, who have felt alienated by well-meaning Christian brothers and sisters. May you read with an open heart and with the realization that I am attempting to be true to my understanding of the radical nature of grace, while also deeply respecting God's love for the institution of marriage.

You will see that I use many examples and illustrations in this book. I have altered identities in these true stories of the many ways individuals can struggle with the painful problems associated with divorce and the healing that can come when we respond to them graciously.

Chapter One

But You Must Have Biblical Grounds!

Pastor James sat behind his massive desk, listening carefully as a longtime member of his church, Michelle, unraveled the story of her crumbling marriage. She was known as a pleasant, soft-spoken woman, and it was out of character for her to speak as directly as she now was about the failure of her marriage. In years past, no one would have known by her demeanor that she felt so persistently dejected and hurt, but now she could cover up no more. This conversation with her pastor was her "coming out," and the story she told was not pretty.

"It's been twenty-three years since Allen and I married, and I can recall very few moments when we were happy or felt connected," Michelle began. "Shortly after our honeymoon, Allen made it clear that he was the boss and we were going to do things his way. It's not like he wrote out a list of rules I had to follow, but he was very opinionated about the way things should be done and he became very easily agitated when I didn't fall in line.

"In the first month, I learned that a wrong move on my part would bring out temperamental outbursts like I had never seen before. Allen would yell at me for the most minor offenses and would punish me with long spells of silence and withdrawal. If I displeased him, even for something as minor as being a few minutes late getting home from the grocery store, he would go into a long tirade and inform me that I owed it to him to be responsible. I eventually learned that he meant I had to live my life exactly as he specified."

The pastor was tracking Michelle's words closely. Gently he asked, "Did you see any hint of this kind of behavior prior to marriage?"

"Well, yes and no. I knew when we dated that he had a reputation for being strongly opinionated. His younger sister once told me that he had a wild temper as a boy, particularly in his teen years. But I never saw that side of him while we dated, so naïvely I just passed it off and didn't look into it any further."

"How has this problem built up over the years?"

"We've had lots of highs and lows," Michelle explained. "I'm not a take-charge person by nature, so I was able to fit myself into his mold a good portion of the time. But I'm not perfect either, so invariably I'd say or do something to set Allen off and he'd go for days into one of his anger spells. I'd say we were lucky if we could make it two or three weeks without his becoming excessively angry. In the last five or six years, the frequency has been much worse, and the intensity of his rages has been so strong that I'm in a constant state of caution. Our lives are miserable. He's told me numerous times that he hates me and that he deserves better than me. I've been insulted and cursed and called every name in the book, and I feel like I've become only a shell of my real self."

Pastor James spoke kindly as he asked, "How do you assess your efforts to be a godly wife?" He wanted to know if she was going to be honest about her flaws or if she was just playing a blame game.

"I'm the first to admit that I have my imperfections," she replied. "All my life I've had a nagging problem of hidden insecurity. People may not see it when I'm in public because I try to keep up a friendly image, but Allen does. He hates how it can negatively affect my relating style."

"For instance?"

"Well, I know that I shouldn't be defensive when he points out an imperfection of mine. For example, I might forget to take a movie back to the rental store on time, or I may be irritable with one of the kids, and Allen will bring those things to my attention. In the early part of our marriage I'd hear those comments, feel guilty, and vow to work on it. For the last several years, I know I've been edgy sometimes when he corrects me because I'm so tired of feeling criticized. I know I shouldn't be thin-skinned, and a lot of the time I am not. But

I *can* be moody, which then causes me to give off the appearance of frustration. I know that doesn't help matters any, but it's part of my humanness."

The pastor and Michelle talked for an hour as she recounted one incident after another when Allen had exploded at her or one of their three children (now eighteen, fourteen, and eleven). She told him that they could go months, sometimes a year, without sexual relations. She recounted holidays and vacations ruined by his ongoing anger and criticism. Family members had expressed concerns that they felt she was in an abusive marriage. Their two older kids, both girls, had cut off virtually all activities with their dad. They said plainly that they did not like him and wished he would leave. Michelle had long ago pulled out of social activities involving other couples because she was also embarrassed by his "loose cannon" remarks. He would go into a tirade after they got home, recounting all the mistakes he thought she'd made. She and Allen had gone to four or five counselors, and each time he would quit when the focus was placed on changes he needed to make.

Michelle looked squarely at her pastor and said, "If I stay in this marriage any longer I'm going to lose whatever feeling of dignity I have left. This man, by his own admission, has no love for me. He has treated me like dirt for over twenty years. He's alienated himself from our kids to the point that all three are asking me to please divorce him. My extended family can't stand him because he's so mean-spirited. I have no hope that anything will change. I'm forty-five years old and I cannot bear the thought of living with him the rest of my life. I've got too much good inside me to allow myself to be treated like this indefinitely."

The pastor looked somberly at her and said, "I can appreciate your frustration. I've known both you and Allen for a long time, and I know that you especially have a reputation as a caring, gentle Christian woman. I'm *very* sorry you're going through this pain."

Michelle was relieved to hear her pastor's words of support. Then he took a deep breath and asked one more question. "There's one thing I need to know before you proceed with any divorce plans. Has there ever been a time in your marriage when you've known Allen to commit adultery?"

Shaking her head, Michelle said, "No, thankfully that's one problem we've not had to face. I honestly think Allen has such a low opinion of women that he'd rather keep his distance from us. If he does have a lust problem, I don't know about it. I can say he's very secretive about his private thoughts, so you never know what's in his mind. As far as I know, though, he's never been with another woman."

Pastor James paused for a moment, stroked his chin slowly and said, "You realize, then, that you have no biblical grounds for divorce. I can plainly see that your marriage is not what God has in mind, and I can see that your life is less than satisfactory because of that. I really do sympathize with your unfortunate circumstances, but you have to understand that I cannot back you if you divorce for reasons that are not clearly consistent with the Bible. The only other provision for divorce is abandonment by an unbelieving spouse, and that's not viable since Allen has professed Christ as his savior."

"But can't you see that we have nothing that resembles a Christian marriage?" Michelle pleaded. "Believe me, I've agonized for years about the ways I could bring Christ more into the center of our lives. Any time I suggest family devotions or prayers, he just accuses me of being falsely pious. He professes to be a Christian, but there's no evidence of God's presence in his life. We've gone to church and to counseling and to marriage conferences, but nothing moves him. He remains as angry and mean as ever, and no discussion will cause him to go in a better direction."

Nodding sympathetically, Pastor James said, "Again, I've got to say that I truly feel sorry that you have such a difficult situation. I certainly wouldn't want to trade places with you. You have to realize that God hates divorce, and only under the strictest of circumstances does He allow Christians to be divorced. Surely you can appreciate the need to follow biblical guidelines."

Clearly flustered, Michelle countered, "I don't think anyone who knows me would doubt my love for the Lord. It's been my goal since I was a child to love and serve God. I think you know me well enough to know the level of my commitment to Him. I wouldn't be making the decision to divorce if the situation were not severe. This man has verbally assaulted me many, many times. He has driven all three of my children to the point of despair, and I fear losing them if something is not done. He's shoved me on several occasions and threatened violence against me. He's even spit into my face twice. Can't you see, I *cannot* continue in this?"

Pastor James's face was a mirror of the frustration he felt. His understanding of scripture put him in the position of having to side against a decent woman who had real complaints about a virtually disintegrated marriage. In his desire to uphold Biblical beliefs, he was missing a great opportunity to minister to one who was clearly in need. So focused was he on being Biblically consistent that he convinced himself a kind or empathic approach would be considered unbiblical. He was caught in the bind of all-or-nothing thinking. After a long pause, he replied, "We can't take the instructions of the Bible lightly. When Jesus spoke the words about divorce, it was His way of saying He wanted marriages to stay together even if it came at a high personal cost. I truly hurt for your situation, Michelle, but you've got to realize that biblical teaching takes priority."

In the months after this conversation, Michelle did indeed go through with the divorce, and it was predictably ugly. Using the same reasoning as their pastor, Allen claimed that Michelle had no biblical right to divorce and used this argument to make life a living nightmare for her. He attempted to win in the court of public opinion by telling friends and acquaintances that although they had problems, there were no true grounds for divorce. In all his discussions with non-family members, he minimized his contributions to the break-up by admitting that he had problems with anger but it was because she was not emotionally balanced. As the divorce was pending, several well-meaning Christian friends talked with Michelle about her reasons for filing legal documents. Just as the pastor had done, they expressed sympathy for her hurt but withheld full support because they could not feel comfortable with her decision.

Michelle's children were old enough to recognize just how miserable their mother was in this marriage. All three openly expressed relief that they would not have to witness their dad's tirades anymore.

They all told her that they wished she had made the move sooner. The eleven-year-old, Todd, was somewhat conflicted because he simply didn't like being from a split family; yet even he said, "Mom, I just can't stand to listen to Dad yelling at you as much as he does. I dread it when he comes home because we all change into fearful people who don't want to do anything to make him mad."

The three children were aware that some Christian friends were perplexed by their mother's decision, and it only caused them to question their capacity for love, especially at a time when it was most needed. Chelsea, the eighteen-year-old, told her mother, "Nobody knows the misery you've lived with except you. If they are going to shun you for getting out of this long-term, abusive relationship, then I don't want anything to do with those people. I think they're all so worried about what makes *them* feel comfortable that they're forgetting that you are a real person with real hurts!" Her insight was right on target.

Michelle's uneasiness about being in a controversy caused her to withdraw from the church almost completely. The children continued with some of their youth activities because they liked being with their friends, but they definitely felt disillusioned because of the confusion some felt regarding their mother. In fact, once Chelsea left later that year for college, she dropped out of church altogether, claiming that she wanted nothing to do with a religious system that could not love her mother through the most difficult trial of her life.

Michelle's plight is not isolated. Certainly she represents a growing number of Christians who are facing the dilemma of what to do in the face of an unworkable marriage. Knowing that some well-meaning friends would challenge her motives, she was laden with both the problem of coming to terms with her new role as a single mom and her lessened status among friends. She had to resign herself to the reality that she had become a controversial figure in many circles.

The sad truth is that people like Michelle need not be placed in such a painful position. Though well meaning, her Christian friends who insisted that Biblical standards be maintained were missing a

much-needed ministry opportunity. Believing that it was good to uphold the highest regard for marriage, they attempted to remain true to
their devotion to Christ even as they missed His spirit of grace. They
ostracized a hurting person who needed their love in large measure.

Unusual Circumstances

At seminars and in my private counseling practice, I have spoken
with hundreds of divorcees or near-divorcees. Virtually all will attest
to one truth: Christians can be confused about how they should respond to those who have divorced. Many ingredients go into the dis-
solving of a marriage: gross insensitivity, control problems, infidelity,
quitting, anger, abuse, mistreatment of children, and just plain meanness. Regardless of the cause or who is most at fault, the divorcee is left
to face the question, "What is wrong with you?" These individuals experience an additional stigma beyond the one secular divorcees face
when their fellow church members treat them as suspicious or questionable characters. For most, this treatment is disillusioning, the kind
of experience for which one can never be fully prepared. It drives
some into emotional despair, possibly for years.

Most of these Christian divorcees are conflicted. They want to
move forward in the confidence that they can continue to be useful
to God. However, they are haunted by the nagging guilt that they
have contradicted the laws of Christianity in order to move from disaster toward healthiness. A high percentage of these people realize
that they have not been able to follow God's perfect plan, but because of the queasiness of some fellow Christians they carry the extra
burden of feeling that they must prove themselves at their most emotionally depleted time.

The stories I have heard about Christians who chose to leave
an unworkable marriage but remained guilt-ridden are heartbreak-
ing. These folks could not produce evidence of biblical grounds for
divorce, despite compelling reasons for divorce. Here are a few examples of what I have heard, each involving a spouse who claimed
to be a true Christian.

- A woman endured for years her husband's rages and dictatorial demeanor. The last straw came when he pinned her against the wall with his forearm to her neck and put a gun to her head, shouting, "I ought to kill you! Do you hear me? One false move and you're dead!" She filed for divorce and brought criminal charges against him; yet despite the common sense of this, she was still questioned by people who insisted that divorce seemed to be a harsh response.

- A man's wife became pregnant, but she declared she was not ready to be a mother. The couple argued heatedly about her desire to have an abortion, with him being strongly opposed to it. Knowing of his strong disapproval, she went through with an abortion alone. The divisiveness of this act was too great, and the marriage dissolved within months.

- A wife found herself amazed after years of marriage that her husband simply had no interest in or willingness to engage in even the simplest forms of interaction. He would work long hours just to stay away from the house. He made it a point to remain distant from her when he was home. Frequently, he would not look at her or speak to her when she attempted to talk with him. He celebrated none of her birthdays or anniversaries; nor did he give her Christmas presents. When she asked to talk about their marriage, he would quietly shrug and say, "There's nothing to discuss." He simply refused to engage with her on the most minimal level—no sex, no social life, no interest in her personal life.

- A woman learned her husband had been engaged for years in questionable business practices; if caught, he could be criminally prosecuted. He had refused to file income taxes and was secretive about everything having to do with money. He did not heed any of her attempts to correct their problems. In fact, he was so controlling with his money that he gave her only a small, fixed allowance each week. Whenever she spent money on anything he deemed unnecessary, he would deduct that amount from the next week's allowance. All the while, he maintained no accountability for the whereabouts of his own money. They shared no common friends and had a loveless life. He expressed no devotion to her and became angry if she ever suggested change. Counseling was completely out of the question for him.

- A wife was hypercontrolling of her husband and children. She rarely smiled but frequently criticized all of them. When her husband made friends, she quickly alienated him from them with her antisocial, harsh behavior. She would openly chastise him in front of their children, telling him frequently he was not fit to be a father because he did not meet her standards. She had an unusually tight relationship with her mother and openly disdained the men in her life, including her father and brothers. The husband jumped through hoops trying to win her favor, but it was never enough. She told him she regretted marrying, yet she would not leave. She made it clear that she would make no adjustments to be different. Her stock reply to his every request for change was, "Just deal with it."

- A husband and wife received some unusual news one day regarding both sets of parents. The in-laws had known each other for years. One evening the husband's father got into a very ugly argument with the wife's father. The conflict became so severe that the husband's father pulled a gun and shot and killed the wife's father. The trauma was horrific, and the couple could not agree about the reasons for the shooting. The tension was so extreme, they divorced.

- A man and woman met through an Internet chat room. For several months they "conversed" with each other and felt they had fallen in love. They met four or five times in person and on an impulse decided to marry. Three years into the relationship, the husband admitted how shallow his original decision had been. "We have nothing in common," he explained. Neither liked the other one. They spent as much time apart as possible, including holidays and vacations. "I have no idea why we married, except that we were each lonely. It was a very foolish decision."

- A man and woman, both widowed, married after a whirlwind romance. Almost immediately the wife told the husband she would have nothing to do with his adult children or his grandchildren. In an almost paranoid way, she claimed she just didn't feel comfortable around them because she assumed they would compare her unfavorably to their mother. Since his family members lived nearby, there were frequent gatherings. Every time the husband talked with her about attending, a major argument would ensue. If the husband chose to visit his family without her, the wife accused him of not loving her. Yet he felt it was absurd to cease all relations with them, which is what would have pacified his wife. They eventually split up because they were unable to go more than a few days at a time without this issue creating major friction.

• A husband had a long history of alcohol and cocaine abuse. He had been through several treatment programs, none producing any cessation of his addictive behavior beyond a month. Having a job with lots of travel, he had little accountability and would submit to no one. Although he could be engaging and friendly, his first priority clearly was to his addictions. He would often stop at a happy hour on the way home from work for "just one beer" but end up staying out until well after midnight. His wife knew not to count on him to help with the kids or to take care of routine family chores because he would either use cocaine or drink beer daily. Nothing had priority over this habit.

I could go on and on with many other examples of marriages that have dissolved because of problems that are not specified in the Bible as reasons for divorce. No doubt you could add a few examples of your own. There is virtually no end to the kinds of trouble in marriages that make them unworkable at best and destructive at worst. In cases such as these, when Christian husbands or wives make the very difficult decision to divorce, they feel rejected by fellow Christians who are unable to feel comfortable with the marital split.

Two primary passages of scripture are, in essence, the source of this discomfort and difficulty:

• "And I say to you, whoever divorces his wife, except for immorality, and marries another woman, commits adultery" (Matthew 19:9).

- "Yet if the unbelieving one leaves, let him leave; the brother or sister is not under bondage in such cases" (I Corinthians 7:15).

Well-intended Christians recognize that these are the only two Biblical reasons to divorce: adultery and abandonment by a non-believing spouse. When confronted with a marriage torn by any problem not specified in the Bible, many feel they are being disloyal to God if they respond too kindly to the divorcee. The need to be Biblically correct can overrule the willingness to display love. Even as they might concede that there are incidents warranting separation, they are still perplexed when the problem crescendos into a full-fledged divorce.

I have found it interesting that many Christians who are on the front lines of counseling in these cases privately confide their discomfort with the awkwardness sometimes produced by adhering to a strict Biblical stand. One minister typified the thoughts of many as he talked with me about a woman who had come under much physical and verbal abuse from her husband. "If she were my sister or daughter," he told me, "I'd want her out of that situation as fast as it could be arranged. But being a pastor, my congregation expects me to remain true to the Bible, so I have to hold the line and say that divorce shouldn't proceed. In this woman's case, it feels as if I'm telling her to remain a punching bag. I've gotten to the point that I just look the other way if someone like her files for divorce. I don't really want to see people remain in a bad situation, but I can't be seen as condoning divorce."

As for the divorcees, they are often left feeling like second-class Christians. They've been forced, through no desire of their own, into what seems like shunning scripture in order to protect themselves from the misery of an ungodly marriage. In my experience with these folks, I have been taken back by the feelings of shame they harbor because they know they have displeased, or at least baffled, Christian friends. Dear friends often cannot come to terms with their divorced friend still being deemed a full-fledged Christian who has much to offer the body of Christ as a divorcee, as they do with married people.

I have heard statements such as these:

"I go to church, and it's amazing that certain people won't talk with me anymore. They won't even look at me!"

"People will try to talk me out of divorcing, yet they know absolutely nothing of the horrors I've lived through."

"It's been suggested that perhaps I'm not really saved."

"I was asked to step down from committees, even though I was the one wronged in the marriage and never wanted the divorce."

"Several people have automatically assumed that I've had an affair or that I might now put the moves on the opposite sex."

"Other parents won't let their kids come to our house anymore because they don't want their children associating with someone from a broken home."

It is time for us to put our hands up and say, "Enough!" Even more, let us proclaim: "If you have been divorced, we can still do business with you. You can still be a full participant in the wonderful love and fellowship of God—and (dare I say it) you may actually have *more* to offer the body of Christ because of your troubled experiences." The greatest wisdom is often the result of suffering and disappointment.

Where does this awkwardness that Christians feel in the face of divorce come from? In my view, the source is the tendency to prioritize correctness over mercy. In a culture that winks casually at the sanctity of marriage, the church *needs* to be an advocate for the home. The church is right to declare that divorce is not God's desire, that marriage vows are meant to be held in the highest regard. At the same time, godly people can know that they are not disobeying scripture when they show empathy and goodness to those who have not been able to maintain a perfect standard. A person can be a strongly committed, sincere Christian and still experience divorce because of unusual and unworkable circumstances. Rather than making judgments about the advisability of divorce proceedings, there are times when Christians can exert the greatest influence on the Lord's behalf by wrapping loving arms around someone who is experiencing one of life's most difficult traumas. Doing so does not necessarily dilute a believer's loyalty to God's laws concerning marital honor.

Yes, I am aware that some people take marriage too lightly. Some may rationalize their divorce in order to maintain a commitment to a shallow, self-absorbed way of life. Sometimes, confrontation or exploration of alternative options may indeed prove helpful. It is always best to acknowledge that lasting marriages are a part of God's perfect plan for husbands and wives, and that divorce should only be used as a last resort. I am also aware, though, that some people have experienced divorce even in an ongoing effort to live appropriately for Christ. To these people, we can extend compassion and godly assistance as we ask, "In the face of this tragedy, how can we help you reaffirm and reclaim your position in God's kingdom?"

To move forward with compassion, we need a clear perspective on Biblical teachings that assist us in our response to marriage and divorce. We are wise to avoid pronouncements that lead to a condemning spirit, just as we are wise to maintain a lofty reverence for God's love of the institution of marriage.

Beginning Assumptions

As you read this book, understand that there are two core beliefs that shape my thoughts and opinions.

First, *neither Jesus nor Paul condemned individuals simply because they missed the mark.* There are those who believe they are being consistent with Jesus and Paul's teachings when they insist upon keeping rules and living with correct performance in order to curry the favor of God. This mind-set was strong in the days of the New Testament. Yet the two people in scripture who most strongly protested against this performance-based thinking within the church were Jesus and Paul. Jesus reserved His harshest rebukes for the people who prided themselves in being religiously correct, who set themselves apart from erring folk, yet who could not live perfectly themselves. He referred to them as vipers and whitewashed sepulchres who are full of hypocrisy and lawlessness (read Matthew 23:1–36). Likewise, the apostle Paul stood firmly against people who entered churches insisting that Christians must live correctly before they could expect God to show favor. Just read his letter to the Galatians if you want to get an idea of his disdain for this mind-set.

It is ironic, then, that many modern Christians would use selected teachings of Jesus and Paul to scrutinize fellow strugglers for the purpose of determining if they can accept them or not. Just as religious people of that day would say, "You must follow these rules to prove your worthiness to God," some people today state that "You have to follow Jesus and Paul's mandates or you will lose favor with God." Given the willingness of both Jesus and Paul to love those who did not match their perfect principles, I assume they would be displeased to know that some Christians use their teachings today to reject other Christians who have failed to do what is right.

Second, *the marriage commitment is to be held in highest regard*. Like virtually all of my Christian cohorts, I am disheartened every time I hear of a fellow believer getting divorced. I don't like divorce. I don't like the potential damage it can do to children. I don't like the strains it places on friendships. I don't like how extended family members are adversely affected by it. The marriage commitment is a powerfully necessary ingredient for a church and a society that want to stand for things that are right and pure and good.

Those who enter divorce proceedings lightly show shallow thinking and are putting themselves in the position of adopting a value system that is relativistic and self-serving. Divorce should be a decision only of last resort and should be accompanied by wise counsel and accountability. I have known many people who chose to divorce even though their mates still wanted to seek growth and reconciliation, and even though wise friends advised that it would be an ill-fated decision. In such a case, I feel frustrated, sometimes to the point of great sadness. I wonder how some people can leave a marriage for weak or superficial reasons. Certainly the Lord knows we are capable of making poor decisions that are based on shallow reasoning, which explains His strong emphasis on maintaining marital vows.

Understand, therefore, as I discuss the notion of grace and divorce, that I do not want to be regarded as someone who gives license or credibility to people who simply are living for self-satisfaction, showing little regard for God's sacred institution of marriage. What I *do* want to prompt you to consider is inclusion of a loving attitude toward divorcees. I want to encourage this particularly when the maximum effort has been made to save a dying marriage, even if the reasons for divorce do not include Biblical grounds but the marriage remains irreparable. When Christians come to the end of an extremely difficult, even ungodly, marriage, the last thing they need is fellow Christians feeding them guilt and shame. Instead, let us be givers of encouragement and kindness. Let us pledge to uphold them as they seek to continue to live under the guidance of the Lord. It is possible to be graceful even as we continue to believe in the fullness of Biblical principles.

Later we will explore Matthew 19 and I Corinthians 7, and explain how these passages are intended to be applied with grace. Before we get to them, though, I will lay a foundation regarding the beginnings of Christian teachings about marriage and divorce. Let's start at the very beginning, with Adam and Eve, because later we will see that Jesus refers His listeners back to that time when He addresses the subject of divorce. Once we've explored a Biblical mindset for reckoning with the problem of divorce, we can then examine how to help Christians address positively the issue of divorce among their friends, family members, and fellow believers.

It is good and necessary to exhort one another regarding scriptural teachings, so long as simultaneously we are willing to be known for grace and acceptance.

Chapter Two

Adam's Nature, God's Grace

There once was a time when a marriage relationship could be experienced with absolutely no conflict, anger, insecurity, or insensitivity. Prior to Adam and Eve's fall into sin, humanity knew no negatives. The Bible offers little about life prior to the Fall, but we can assume that the first husband and wife exchanged rewarding doses of kindness, understanding, affection, and contentment. One will existed, God's will, and both Adam and Eve lived in accordance with His desire for their lives.

"From the fruit of the trees of the garden you may eat freely," Adam was told, "but from the fruit of the Tree of Knowledge of Good and Evil you shall not eat, lest you die" (see Genesis 2:16–17). In this initial instruction, God laid out the blueprint for a healthy life. First, He affirmed that He was giving Adam and all humans who would follow the gift of freedom. They had the privilege to choose how they would live. Adam's one restriction was that he could not eat of the Tree of Knowledge of Good and Evil. By stating this, God was in essence saying, "Keep in mind as you make each free choice that I have already established what is right and wrong. This arena needs no adjustment. It's fixed. It cannot be improved. So in wisdom, Adam, filter every one of your free choices through My definition of right and wrong. Don't make any attempt to play God."

For a period of time—how long we do not know—Adam and Eve lived according to this initial instruction. They carried on their existence in paradise, surely experiencing what we now know to be the fruit of the Spirit: love, joy, peace, patience, kindness, goodness, faithfulness, gentleness, and self-control. Life surely was a delight.

Satan, however, was not far away. He watched Adam and Eve carefully, surely feeling insulted and greatly displeased that God would have created creatures bearing His image to subdue the earth and have dominion over it. Being ever-defiant against God, Satan yearned to bring down His people, so he devised a scheme. He saw that the husband and wife experienced joy and contentment, and he also recognized that they were quite proud of their healthy sense of satisfaction and pleasure with life. (We still have the capacity for this positive form of pride today.) Drawing from his own experience of rebellion against God, Satan well knew that pride could take on a completely different dimension, one that pits humanity against God. So he went to work.

Focusing first on Eve, and suspecting that through her he could pull Adam down, he began speaking words of flattery. He hooked her at her place of positive pride. "Do I understand that you've been denied access to the trees of the garden?" His exaggerated question was intended to cause Eve to question God's good provision for them, and to think highly of the reasoning she applied in pondering that question.

"Actually, no, that's not the case," she replied. "We've been told that we can eat from all of the trees, with the exception of the one in the middle, which we can't eat from or touch." (Actually God had said nothing about touching it; Eve was flustered.)

Satan appealed again to her pride, but this time with a wicked twist. "What do you mean, you can't eat of that tree?" He wanted her to think, "Hey, yeah. He's got a good point. Why would God put a restriction like that on me? After all, I am a good person. I'm smart. I have common sense. Surely God doesn't want me to live my life unnecessarily restricted."

Satan let a moment go by as Eve considered that point, and then he added: "You know, you're not going to die. If you eat of the Tree of Knowledge of Good and Evil, you'll share God's wisdom. You will know ultimate correctness and you'll be Godlike yourself! Imagine that!" (See Genesis 3:1–5.)

At this point, Eve's positive pride began changing into self-preoccupation. As she considered the possibility of being equal to

God, she became full of her own self-absorbed preferences, cravings, and desires. She contemplated what it would be like to be in
control, to have no restraints at all. The allure was so strong that
she ate of the tree, and pulled Adam into doing the same thing. Because of their pride and self-absorption, both fell from the paradise
in which they had lived.

Let's understand fully that this familiar story is not about two
people getting into some bad apples. It is about the fundamental
change of character that occurred inside the spirits of Adam and Eve,
and through them to all of us who followed. Where once they had
yielded to God's perfect will, they now decided to follow their own
separate wills: "I'm in control. I'll call the shots, thank you. I have the
final say of what is right and what is wrong." Self-centeredness became the defining characteristic of human personality.

Now, consider a broad idea that can be taken from this story.
You and I, being "in Adam," have the same core characteristic of
self-absorbed pride at the base of our personalities. We are filled with
it. This trait is so pervasive that *every* negative trait in your personality can be traced to the influence of sinful pride. Self-absorption
can be observed in such openly harsh, negative qualities as criticism,
manipulation, irritability, rejection, insults, rebellion, lying, edgi-
ness, insulting, and being argumentative. Sinful pride can be seen in
other negative, but less harsh, traits such as worry, defensiveness,
phoniness, insecurity, and gossip. Sinful pride can also lurk in the
midst of more passive traits: punishing withdrawal, pouting, ignoring, refusing to speak, laziness, procrastination, giving half-hearted
effort, being cold, being unreliable, chronic forgetfulness, sexual pre-
occupation, and denial.

Being absorbed with self and intrinsically prone to live contrary
to God's pronouncements of right and wrong, we see virtually no
end to these prideful traits. They are indigenous to human nature,
and they are contrary to God's ideal for successful living. Our personalities are thoroughly infected with pride.

Besides pride and all it brings with it, Adam and Eve's sin also
brought them death. God had said they would die if they disobeyed
Him, so at that point He could have ended their lives. But instead of

executing judgment immediately, God did something unexpected. First, He let them know that they could continue to live, but with consequences. He explained that each would experience personal strain, to remind them (and all who followed) that a life of disobedience to God is less than easy. This is as true today as it was then; we cannot expect events to unfold in a way that produces perfect results. Pain exists. Strain is part of what we must experience.

Second, once God explained these consequences to Adam and Eve, He then did something very strange. He took an animal (perhaps a sheep?) and killed it right before them. He tanned the animal, and then taking its skin He placed it on the nude bodies of the two for them to wear as clothing (Genesis 3:21). What is the symbolism of this act?

God was communicating to Adam and Eve (and to all who followed) that though they would die, for the time being He was suspending the death sentence and accepting a substitute in their place. Even at this early moment in human history He knew that in the course of time he would commission His son, Jesus Christ, to die in their stead. The slaying of the animal, then, can be understood as a foreshadowing of that future event. God's nature is to love, and He so desired to embrace humanity that He was willing to show mercy rather than execute immediate judgment for their sinfulness. The precedent for grace—love that is not earned or deserved—was established in this scene.

Years later, when their sons, Cain and Abel, were of age and ready to pledge their loyalty to God, Abel fully accepted the doctrine of substitutionary death. He offered God the sacrifice of his flock's firstborn, and God was pleased. Cain, in contrast, brought God the first of his crops, representing the works of his hand. Not impressed by a sacrifice of mere human works with no substitutionary death, God disregarded this offering. Filled with pride, Cain displayed his arrogance by killing Abel, the one who was anchored in the grace of God. He had no appreciation for the concept of grace.

Centuries later, when Jesus was questioned about his opinion of divorce, He referred twice to "in the beginning." That being the case, it is necessary for us to understand the implications of our first family's relationship with God. It sets the stage for a broader understanding of Jesus' later teachings.

Lessons from Adam's Beginnings

The first lesson is that *God's earliest standard for humanity was perfection.*

In today's world, we have so much imperfection that we can hardly comprehend a perfect life. All the disease, crime, emotional imbalance, and conflict that we now experience had no place in God's original design. We must remind ourselves that the ongoing struggles of humanity are part of an interim experience sandwiched between God's gift of paradise to the first humans and God's gift of eternal glory with Him once sin has run its course. Much of what we experience now is outside God's perfect desires for us. By virtue of sin's repercussions, we know pain and failure. This dilemma is ongoing and has invaded every fabric of life. But let's not forget: it is temporary.

Allow yourself to ponder for a moment the idyllic life God planned for Adam and Eve. Creation scientists tell us that the earth's conditions prior to the Fall were so pure that these two experienced the ultimate in fitness and health. Their perfect bodies knew no disease. Their temperaments were most pleasing. Their communication was unblemished. Their thoughts were pure. Surely each radiated joy, encouragement, and love.

Have you ever known of a marriage completely void of conflict? I certainly have not. Consider, though, that prior to sin Adam and Eve never argued. They could find constructive and loving solutions in life together. They took delight in serving each other. Their "one flesh" experience was fully synchronized and uplifting. They thought only good thoughts. They were bonded in a mutual love for their Creator.

God wanted nothing but perfection for the original ones He made in His image. This has not changed; He still wants the finest for us. As He revealed His plan of redemption to humanity through scripture, He inspired biblical writers repeatedly to uphold His perfect standard. The Bible is not wishy-washy in its instructions because it is the representation of God's mind. It is a reflection of who He is. As a simple illustration, scripture does not say, "Be somewhat nice, every now and then, if you feel like it." It states, "Be kind to one another, tenderhearted, and forgiving one another." The message is pure, with no hedging or compromise. That's the way God thinks. Perfection is His will for us now just as it was in Adam's time, and just as it will be in heaven.

The second lesson is that *God gave humankind the freedom to choose how they would conduct their lives*.

The more I contemplate the genius of God, the more amazed I am that He considered every detail necessary for a life of fullness and completion. One astonishing idea of His is free choice. Wanting humans to have the broadest ability to appreciate all that He is, God realized that an automatic, robotic love for Him would not suffice. When He created a perfect earth and set in motion a perfect scheme of right and wrong, He gave humanity the privilege to choose if it would indeed blend its ways with His plan. The risk existed that humanity would choose counter to His plan; but that risk, by definition, had to exist in order for freedom to be freedom. Chosen obedience is far superior to forced compliance.

When I talk with people about the possibility of freedom in each person's life, I get mixed reactions. Some people, weary of mandated living, heave a sigh of relief and say, "Tell me more." They yearn for a life of choices, and they can envision the good that could result. Others, though, are less enthusiastic about the notion of freedom. They ask, "Do you realize the problems that could result if everyone decided just to be free? That could lead to chaos or anarchy, and I want nothing to do with that!"

Freedom, indeed, is a mixed blessing. I once heard a well-known cleric state that "Freedom is defined as the responsibility to live as you ought." I could appreciate his sentiment, but I had to conclude that his definition was incorrect. He was describing what he hoped people would do with their freedom, and in doing so he was denying its essence. Simply put, freedom is the privilege of choices. Some use their freedoms responsibly, and some do not. Though we often don't like what people do with their freedom, nevertheless it has been a reality since God first spoke to Adam.

As we will explore in greater detail in pages to come, Jesus affirmed human freedom each time he taught grace. He realized that God did not remove free will from Adam and Eve after they had chosen rebellion against God. Instead, He offered grace and allowed them to continue making choices about how they would live, knowing He would continue loving them even amid poor choices. Consequences for each choice were put into place; they are some of the issues we explore later as they relate to divorce.

To make freedom less risky for New Testament believers, God added the gift of the Holy Spirit. Realizing our propensity to use freedom in the wrong ways, God commissioned the Holy Spirit to guide and instill conviction in us regarding our daily decisions. In a sense, we can say the Holy Spirit is a hedge against irresponsible, unbridled freedom. As we yield to His teaching, we can be saved from the self-absorbed, prideful qualities that accompany our Adamic nature.

The third lesson is that *God's mercy overrides His judgment.*

As I talk with people who have experienced divorce, I hear one story after another of those they know who apparently appoint themselves to be the keepers of the law. They dutifully correct those they determine to be out of God's will. When I hear of Christians correcting other Christians, I am neither completely opposed to the idea nor in favor of it. There are numerous biblical teachings calling for Christian brothers and sisters to hold each other to high standards. We are told to be bold in preaching the word, to exhort one another, to speak truth in love, to be unwavering in our faith. There is no Christian who is so well rounded that accountability and straight-talking friends are unnecessary. We need constant reminders of God's wonderful truth.

My discomfort comes as I witness well-intentioned people so bent on correcting a fellow believer that they lose the ability to love.

Even worse, they risk hindering the work that the Holy Spirit can ultimately do. As an illustration, I recall talking with one man whom I will refer to as Matthew. He learned that his wife had lived a duplicitous life for years. In their marriage, she was aloof at best toward her husband, and at the end of their marriage she admitted to him that she had never loved him. She said she had reluctantly married him under her mother's pressure because he was both kind and financially stable. Though she had let him assume otherwise, prior to marriage she was quite promiscuous. She would later ridicule him for being so foolish to think that she was an innocent young lady in need of a caring, moral man. In their years together, she repeatedly maxed out credit cards buying luxuries for herself. She looked for the party scene wherever it could be found and mocked his conservatism. She openly admitted not wanting to be married, yet refused to seek counseling. She brazenly told him the main reason for her staying with him was her lack of desire to go back to work. After many discussions about how they might try to blend their needs, Matthew's final straw came when his wife left home on Christmas day to get drunk with a single friend of hers who had no family in town.

As Matthew agonized about the viability of keeping the marriage together, his wife flippantly told him, "You know I'm not going to change, so you're going to have to learn to be more like me." When he discussed divorce with her, she finally conceded: "Well, I've been wondering when you'd get around to doing it." Matthew knew she had never intended to be a loyal wife.

Once word got out that the two had separated, an associate minister from the church called and told Matthew he was not allowed to divorce his wife unless there were biblical reasons. He then asked if there was any unfaithfulness. Matthew's reply was tactful: "If you don't mind, I'd rather not go into the details because I have no desire to enter into a potential smear campaign." Matthew barely knew the minister casually and had never had a serious conversation with him. "You realize that I have to report to the church's board of elders," came the minister's reply, "and if you can't give us a good reason for the divorce, we won't be able to allow you to take communion or vote as a member of the church on any business matters."

The last thing Matthew needed to hear from this distant acquaintance was words of rejection from church fellowship. He told me, "I had never been so low in my life. I had every intention of calling some men in the church to seek their guidance; but after two separate conversations with this fellow, I vowed never to set foot in that church again. I realized then that I was of value to them only to the extent that I would live within their parameters."

This situation occurred several years ago. Interestingly, I recently learned that this same minister went through a divorce, though I do not know why. I have often wondered if he would respond differently if he were to meet Matthew today.

When God told Adam he could eat freely from the trees of the garden, He also said not to eat of the Tree of Knowledge of Good and Evil. Clearly, then, God and God alone is to be the sole and ultimate arbitrator of justice. He leaves individuals with the responsibility to choose for themselves if they will adhere to His ways, living a life of submission to His control. But no human—pastor or otherwise—is meant to approximate God's ultimate judgment.

It is only normal for Christians who love each other to want God's best for fellow believers. This is why we have formal times of preaching, teaching, discussion, and counseling. We would be remiss if we never spoke truth to each other, even if hearing the truth may hurt. Yet there is a delicate line that we are not to cross, as we need to stay out of the way of the Holy Spirit so He can accomplish His work. Ultimately, we can aid in getting the message out, but we run the risk of great arrogance when our words are accompanied by coercion and judgment. It is the Holy Spirit, not we, who is to bring conviction to one struggling to make a right decision.

I do believe in the concept of church discipline and withdrawal of fellowship at prescribed times. But I see scripture encouraging it only in extreme cases of "in your face" sins. In every instance, we are ultimately to let each individual (after sound teaching) decide how to submit to God. (Confrontation and discipline are explored more fully in a later chapter.)

The fourth lesson is that *humanity proved incapable of living up to God's perfect standard.*

God knew the risk He was taking in allowing Adam and Eve the freedom to make their own choices. The possibility existed that they would fail the test and choose a life contradictory to God's best desires and laws. This is exactly what happened, and it continues to occur every day in the life of each sinner, no matter how strong the desire to be godly.

Whereas the life of Adam and Eve prior to sin consisted of perfect emotions, intentions, and communications, the opposite became the norm after the Fall. The Genesis account shows how the two immediately experienced defensiveness, blame, isolation, fear, insecurity, guilt, shame, and inferiority. They surely felt anger—especially Cain, who killed his brother.

Today, the same tension continues in every human. None of us is able to escape the grip of sin as we struggle with the very same emotions that Adam and Eve experienced. The apostle Paul summarized this tension for all of us in admitting he often wished to do what was right, only to fail and do the very thing he did not want to do (Romans 7:14–24).

One distinguishing feature of the sin nature is the fact that it plays out differently in each sinner. For instance, one man openly scorned people who were divorced because he could not accept their lack of obedience to God; yet, he himself was ejected from baseball games three times in one season for angrily yelling at his son's coaches. Likewise, he had virtually no relationship with his own college-age daughter after she fell into a lifestyle of drug abuse and promiscuity. Being a divorcee apparently rated lower on the sin scale than being a belligerent parent, so in this man's mind he was still qualified for church fellowship though divorcees were not.

In God's mind, sin is sin. James's letter tells us that a person guilty of one portion of the law is deemed guilty of the total law (James 2:10). God knows that although the sins of one person differ from those of another, we are all in the same boat. The cost of each sin differs, yet the character of each person is so tainted that no one can claim superiority over another.

Allow me to illustrate. In late summer of 1972, like the vast majority of Americans I was enthralled by Mark Spitz's astounding performance in winning seven gold medals in Olympic swimming. No one has since exceeded that record, and it is doubtful anyone will. Arguably, he is the greatest competitive swimmer of all time.

Let's set up an imaginary scenario in which Spitz is challenged by me, Les Carter, to a mammoth swimming race. Standing on the edge of California's Pacific shores, we are going to race to see who can swim to Japan first. On your mark, get set, go!

Not a great swimmer, I trudge along doing the American crawl, then the side stroke, and back stroke, trying to pace myself. But alas, I tire and finally raise my arm, signaling for the boat to pick me up. Spitz, on the other hand, outperforms me from the very beginning. With that Olympic form still intact, his stroke is smooth and his superior conditioning allows him to outdistance me to the extent that I cannot even see him. Nonetheless, in time he too tires and the boat picks him up as well.

After the botched race, let's suppose we create a map as large as the side of a building. On the right side of the map we see California, and on the left is Japan. We place a straight pin on the map showing the location of the places where Spitz and I were rescued. In that huge expanse of ocean, the pins are so close together that it looks as though we are right next to each other; certainly neither of us came close to reaching the ultimate goal. From my limited perspective as a participant in the race, it appears that he was far better than I, but put in the overall perspective his superiority got him virtually no closer to the goal than I was.

We can apply this analogy in considering the errors and misjudgments of one Christian compared to another. When someone divorces, for instance, it seems easy to conclude there is a distinct spiritual inadequacy in that person, compared to a happily married husband or wife. From the human perspective, we might rate them differently. But from the eternal perspective, both married and divorced are so vastly short of God's standard of perfect righteousness that any differences between the groups are irrelevant. We may each be different, yet we are all the same.

If, then, we Christians choose to ostracize the divorcees among us, we first need to be certain that we are perfect according to all the other teachings of the Bible. According to the standard of perfect righteousness, we would have to be free from lust, strong anger, a divisive spirit, lack of forgiveness, fear, deception, double-mindedness, and a whole host of other sins. But that will never happen since no one is close to perfection. (Hence, the need for Christ's atonement on behalf of every one of us.) It is a guarantee that we all fall woefully short of the mark.

The fifth lesson is that God, *through grace, decided to continue with us humans despite our intransigence.*

When most people read the story of Adam and Eve, they tend to hurry past the part of God covering them with the skin of an animal, despite this being one of the most powerful symbols in scripture. Upon witnessing the very first sin, God rightly could have stated, "Look, I told you what the deal would be; we had an agreement. You've crossed the line, so My efforts with you are finished. You're gone." He *could* have, but He did not. Despite their sin against Him, God wanted to continue loving them.

Knowing that His perfect holiness could not commingle with sin's unholiness, God devised a plan that would still make it possible for the first man and woman to commune with Him. He would accept a substitute death, a perfect specimen who would die on their behalf. As the sinners acknowledged their unworthiness to approach God but appealed to His mercy by offering a substitute in their place, God would receive them still. Significantly, the first sacrifice was not accomplished by Adam or Eve, but by God. He is the one who slew the animal and covered the humans in its skin. This, of course, was His way of foreshadowing how He would eventually provide the completely perfect sacrificial lamb in the person of His own Son, Jesus Christ.

God's love is so central to His character that He did all He could to offer a way for us humans to be restored to Him. His grace superseded His law in the time of Adam, just as it does today. God's original law remains as true as ever; we are not to attempt to be like God. Nonetheless, then as now He gives grace higher priority.

Grace Is a Risk

When Christians today reject divorced Christians, they risk giving the law priority over grace. They cling to the principles spoken by Jesus with such tenacity that they miss a golden opportunity to show grace. They wound rather than heal.

After speaking with many people who find it difficult to accept those who do not have Biblical grounds for choosing divorce, I suspect I understand why the vast majority do not find grace easy. They are afraid that if they are forthcoming with grace and mercy, many will interpret it as permission to divorce for poor reasons. This would encourage a *real* epidemic of divorces. In their view, extending grace could lead to reckless liberalism. Indeed, this is a problem that needs to be seriously pondered, but perhaps not in the way you might think.

What is grace if not liberality? By its very nature, grace is not logical, and it can certainly take priority over hard laws. This does not minimize or mock justice but demonstrates just how essential love is to the character of God. None of us—married, divorced, or single—deserves God's grace. None of us! Yet, God takes each person at his or her point of unrighteousness and declares, "Despite your inability to measure up to My perfect standard, I will continue to love you and bless your life. You belong to Me."

Many sincere Christians will say, "Oh, I'm willing to still love divorcees. They can still come to our church. But I can't condone divorce, nor do I believe divorcees should be in leadership because that would be counter to scripture." To that I say, "You've missed the point! No one lives up to scripture!" We cannot arbitrarily exclude some but not others. Yes, in the case of believers who blatantly continue in ongoing immorality, there is a need to remove them from positions of influence in the hope that they will become more attuned to God's truth. Most Christian divorcees, however, do not fit the category of moral or spiritual degenerate. Some do, but I would say most do not. Many divorcees do not want to be divorced at all. They find themselves in that situation from choices made by a spouse who would not cooperate in finding solutions to personal problems or marital needs.

A divorcee's failure is out in the open for all to see, whereas the failure of other Christians may be more hidden. Open or hidden, each Christian has failures, and each requires the same provision of grace and mercy.

As we will explore in later chapters, Jesus made references to God's standards in the beginning, so you must be well grounded in God's position with Adam as you attempt to fully understand Christ's pronouncements. But before we examine Christ's statements, let's go further in understanding the introduction of the law and its purpose in God's plan for us. This we do in the next chapter.

Chapter Three

Enter the Law

When I consider the need for a code of laws, I can't help thinking about family life with small children. Toddler-aged boys and girls can be cute and fun, but they are also oblivious to the needs and perspectives of others. They enter the world bearing Adam's nature; they are naturally predisposed to be prideful and consumed with the self's cravings and desires, which leads to their assumption that they are at the center of the universe and want to be in complete control of their world.

Parents love their little children and naturally want them to experience the greatest number of fulfilling moments in their lives. Knowing that chronic self-absorption is ultimately not fulfilling, parents teach them how to rein in selfishness, directing them to a way of life that is more orderly and respectful of others' needs. In short, parents institute good and necessary laws and consequences that are an extension of the parents' loving intentions.

The stories of Adam and Eve's descendants told in the first books of the Bible make clear that God devoted much effort to reining in their sinful nature. Every time they were lawless and disrespectful of God and became self-absorbed, God would find ways to correct them. In Noah's time, all of humanity (except Noah and his family) was destroyed in a great flood. Soon those descendants lost that lesson as well, as they sought to build a tower that would reach heaven—the Tower of Babel—to demonstrate their godlike wisdom. God separated all those people from one another and sent them to the ends of the earth to correct their false impression of their power. In time, God's favor fell upon Abraham and his descendants, whom He designated

His chosen people and through whom God would reveal His messages of righteousness and redemption to all the other peoples of the world. Abraham's descendants, as you recall, eventually ended up as slaves in Egypt and had to be rescued, under the leadership of Moses.

When the Israelites left Egypt, God planned for them to travel to Canaan, a land of milk and honey where they would live as free people. But God knew they needed laws to help them live their new identity as His representatives to the other peoples of the earth. Just as parents give toddlers specific laws to curtail their natural predisposition to be self-absorbed, God wanted to establish in this fledgling nation a mind-set that would cause them to focus on His ways, not humanity's self-absorbed ways. He would not allow humans to return again to prior forms of lawlessness.

Parents have to think on behalf of their children on an array of subjects; so too God was far reaching in addressing many aspects of life that required His imprint. Through His spokesman, Moses, He addressed how the infant nation should worship God, how property rights should be honored, how family life should unfold. He carefully taught how the specifics of morality should be handled and how to deal with civil and criminal problems. He even gave mandates about matters of personal hygiene as well as what to eat, how to prepare foods, and how to manage family life appropriately. The Mosaic Law in Exodus, Leviticus, and Deuteronomy is vast and quite specific, touching on virtually every component of life.

Included in Moses' pronouncements was a teaching about divorce. It should come as no surprise that human relations among the Hebrew people continued to include prideful behavior that led to marital breakdown. This was not what God wanted, but just as He gave detailed laws for other personal failures He addressed how divorces should proceed. Specifically, divorce was to represent a complete severance of the relations between the husband and wife. If she found disfavor in his eyes because of some form of indecency (not specified), then he should draw up official papers of divorce and release her. She could remarry, but if that marriage also failed she was not allowed to return to the first husband; that would be an "abomination before the Lord" (Deuteronomy 24:1–4).

Clearly, through other scriptures we know that God did not like divorce (just as He did not like stealing, lying, murder, uncleanness, and all other human imperfections). Despite His dislike for it, though, He made room for it, so long as it proceeded in an orderly fashion.

It is important to realize that the Mosaic Law did not arise for arbitrary reasons. God was not in a mood just to begin spelling out regulations for the mere purpose of telling people what to do. He gave humanity free will and witnessed how unrestrained free will coupled with sinful pride repeatedly resulted in disarray. His love was too strong to allow confusion to reign indefinitely, so as a loving Father directing His young He gave His people a structure that they otherwise would not have if left to their own devices.

By giving the Law, He was reminding His people of the first instruction given to Adam: he was free to eat of the trees of the garden with the exception of the Tree of Knowledge of Good and Evil. Now, in great detail, God would spell out what that knowledge entailed.

As we continue to lay a groundwork to help in understanding Jesus' comments on divorce, let's focus on several truths about God's pronouncement of the Mosaic Law.

The first is that *the Law assumed ongoing imperfection*.

If God had known that humans would have eventually been able and willing to correct their prideful ways, He would not have given the Law, but He would simply have let time run its course. As an analogy, there are times when parents watch how their sons act rowdy or rude, but they look on in amusement and say to each other, "Boys will be boys." They don't get overly anxious because they know the children will grow out of it.

God did not operate with such a bemused attitude because He knew better. He knew He could allow millennia to pass and sinners not only would not improve but would revert to the anarchy that existed just prior to Noah's flood. This was an eventuality He was determined to thwart. He did not trust human nature to voluntarily correct itself.

I recall speaking with a woman (we'll call her Sarah) who had accepted Christ as her Savior in her late twenties. Prior to this experience, she had many experiences of alcohol abuse and sexual promiscuity, not to mention all the coy and manipulative attitudes that went along with those misbehaviors. After becoming a Christian, she felt tremendous relief because she now had a blueprint for living that seemed far more trustworthy than the self-oriented lifestyle she had previously known. She went to Bible studies, attended inspiring worship services, and made a whole new set of clean-cut friends. Yet Sarah privately confessed to me that she felt she had not progressed very far as a Christian because she still struggled with the sinful urges of anger, lust, and fear.

You see, Sarah mistakenly assumed that once she learned the core tenets of her new Christian faith, she would no longer be prone to sin-based urges. I told her that although reform was a lofty goal, she need not be shocked when sin recurred in her thoughts and behaviors. I discussed with her the nature of pride and how it manifested in many ways, some blatant and others subtle. I told her that as long as she remained on this side of heaven, she would see evidence of it. Her salvation experience was called justification, being made right before God on the basis of the substitutionary work of Jesus on her behalf. Once received into heaven, she would experience *glorification*, being made perfectly whole. In the meantime, she could experience *sanctification*, maturing toward Christ's likeness. She need not put herself under the impossible expectation of being perfect right now.

Likewise, the Law was given in Moses' time not to finally make people perfect but to keep them focused on a better alternative to self-absorption. The Law presumed an ongoing tendency toward pride, which is why it so specifically spelled out "Do this" and "Don't do that." God did not expect that the Law would put an end to sin and imperfection, but it would at least keep His people from anarchy.

Today, some church people seem to operate with the notion that if people can be properly told what is right and what is wrong, they should be expected to cease from sin's influence and its negative fallout—as if they were saying, "Now that we've told you what you're not supposed to do, we expect that you won't do it." This is both idealistic and naïve. It also is a formula for extending guilt beyond constructive purposes as it weighs sinners down with an impossible expectation of how their lives had better turn out.

It is reasonable to expect that as individuals are trained to know God's ways of right and wrong there should be some evidence that the training is making a positive difference. Presumably, God expected the Hebrew people to live according to a higher standard once the Law was clearly taught. Indeed, He would express anger and disappointment when they behaved godlessly. In a similar manner, it is fair to say that today's Christians should be held to higher standards than people in the secular world, but this should be done with the realization that perfection will not be achieved. God expected improvement but not complete perfection from the people of Moses' day, and the same can be said of Bible-taught Christians today. We should not be shocked and amazed at human failings even as we spur one another toward more faithful behavior.

The second truth is that *the Law showed humans what is required to be deemed special by God.*

When God was preparing the Hebrew people to receive His Law, He gave a conditional promise that can open our understanding for His issuing of the Law in the first place. He told the people, through Moses, "Now, therefore, if you will indeed obey My voice and keep My covenant, then you shall be a special treasure to Me above all people" (Exodus 19:5).

In the centuries prior to Moses, humans (deluded by sinful pride) allowed themselves to think they were special, so special that they had the ability to determine for themselves ultimate right and wrong. This egotistical attitude led to personal ruin; nonetheless, it persisted and showed no sign of abating. By issuing the Law with its many requirements detailing how to be righteous, God was proclaiming: "I am going to show you what it takes for you to be special. Rather than living according to your own self-absorbed ways, I will require that you learn an orderly manner of life where all is just and civil. Once you show yourselves capable of maintaining My standards, you will have earned the designation of God's special treasure." God then gave a standard that was so detailed that it ensured no one would attain it. His point was: "You may think you are special, but I've got news for you. Specialness in My sight consists of perfect holiness, covering every aspect of life."

When I talk with divorcees about their feelings of frustration over being imperfect, I commonly hear the complaint, "As much as I've wanted to live in ways that would cause God to be pleased, I have to admit that I just don't make the grade." To the divorcee, it can seem as though he or she has earned spiritual demerits, leading to struggles with low self-esteem and a host of emotional problems that accompany poor self-assessment. In a high percentage of cases, divorcees retreat into dejection and defeat. No good purpose is served by such self-judgment. A self-deprecating spirit is anchored in the misguided assumption that people have to succeed in keeping all of God's Law, and in failing to do so they are out of favor with Him.

One longtime Christian, Amy, had the misfortune of experiencing divorce not once but twice. In neither case was she the instigator of the marital separation; she told me that she had been willing to make adjustments in each relationship, yet that willingness was not reciprocated. In both divorces, allegations of sexual misconduct were present, but no hard evidence existed that could prove it.

"My problem with all this," she told me, "is that I feel very guilty for making marital decisions that backfired. It certainly makes me look like I'm not stable in my relationship skills, and I don't think I'll ever be received as confidently by people at church. They're nice to me, but I feel like I'm now less credible as a Christian. Sometimes I wonder exactly what God thinks about me too because I know that He must be really disappointed."

As I got to know Amy, I learned she had a deep history of being moral and responsible. She had been well grounded as a youth in Christian teachings, and her training showed in the sense that she treated people well and prioritized service and kindness. In each marriage, she was hardly angelic, yet her negatives seemed no more extreme than most other Christians she knew, and she always remained willing to receive input for growth.

"People who have known me for a long time have been very supportive of me," Amy explained. "They know that I try to exhibit good character and that I'm flexible. Despite their encouragement, though, I can't shake the feeling that I've lost ground in their eyes. I hear the words that God loves me and that He'll never give up on me, but sometimes it just doesn't make my embarrassment go away."

I explained to her: "Anyone who has been a Christian for any length of time knows that a lifestyle ethic is part of the package. We're taught that there are plenty of shoulds and oughts and musts that accompany our relationship with Christ. It's true that followers of Christ really can expect to act and feel differently from nonbelievers because our focus can be more fixed on traits like forgiveness and love."

Tying this thought to her predicament, I said: "A problem often arises in Christians who focus so heavily on living correctly that they link their specialness to God to their ability to live flawlessly. It is true that when we apply the Christian ethic appropriately, God is pleased, yet He is never so dismayed when we fail that He ceases to love us. Christ is the only one who kept God's Law perfectly, so Christ is the only one who can truly claim the title of Most Favored. You and I will never attain that status by our own efforts, but the core message of Christianity is that we don't have to rely on law keeping to find favor with God. As we accept Christ as our intermediary, God sees us with the same goodness as He sees Him."

When God gave the conditional provision of keeping the Law in order to be known as a special treasure, He did so knowing people would not live up to their end of the covenant. He made the Law so thorough and exacting that there was no way any human could be certain of maintaining His favor through perfect works. Either this was a cruel joke He was playing on His people or it signified that He had more to reveal at a later time after it became abundantly obvious that His Law was out of human reach.

Let's underscore that the giving of the Law was a challenge to an arrogant, self-absorbed group of people. Keep in mind that after the

Hebrews' delivery from Egypt and prior to the giving of the Law, the majority of them were grumbling about God's provisions and expressed the idea that God did not know what He was doing. In other words, they were resorting to the age-old prideful belief that they were equal to God. By issuing the Law, God appeared to be saying: "For ages, you people have assumed that you'd do a good job of defining what is right and what is wrong, but you've mostly just bellowed a lot of hot air. Now I'm going to show you exactly what it takes for you to prove that you are indeed as special as you say you are. Here it is, down to the last detail!" He wanted people to realize that being truly special was no minor effort, and they should think carefully if they were to assume they could call themselves righteous.

In retrospect, we now know that God was already planning on sending Christ as His emissary to live the Law to perfection, thus establishing Himself as the One who could act as the intercessor to God. Living the Law would make any person a special treasure, but only Christ could be that special treasure. Christ's message to believers would be, "Because God sees Me as special, if you align with Me, I'll see that He values you in the same fashion. You will be covered by My perfection before God."

The apostle Paul explained (in Romans 5:20) that "the Law came in that the transgression might increase; but where sin increased, grace abounded all the more." His teaching recognized that perfection had to be spelled out clearly in the Law so seekers of God would clearly understand the difference between right and wrong. Knowing clearly what God expects and then admitting an inability to master His expectations in total, we are made ready to receive the rest of God's offering, the gift of grace.

People like Amy, who assume they must live correctly in order to be deemed acceptable to God, have missed the most important message of the Law. God issued the Law to point humans toward perfection, and He also knew He would provide Jesus, who would fulfill the Law on our behalf so that believers, *through Him*, could still claim the status of being God's special treasure. The giving of the Law was one large piece of the puzzle that would eventually help us see grace!

A third truth is that *the Law redirected humans back to perfection, as best as it could be done.*

When parents teach their children the rules of right and wrong, they know the children will fail, but they still want them to stick to the standard as best as they can. Similarly, when God gave the Hebrews the Law with full knowledge they would fail, He wanted them to aim for a lofty standard anyway. It was far better to be imperfect while trying to implement the Law than to quit and say, "It doesn't matter because I can't achieve it any way I try."

We Christians today can find comfort in knowing that we are completely covered by grace, meaning we admit we cannot achieve God's standard. Nonetheless, this does not excuse any of us from ceasing the effort to maintain God's ideals. When I talk with people like Amy and explain I am willing to be gracious toward those who have divorced, I often receive a conflicted response. The message back to me is: "But I have failed. It feels too convenient for me to just claim that I can receive grace and go on my merry way." We can be so conditioned by our culture to perform for acceptance that it can seem too easy to accept God's mercy with no requirements attached.

In a sense, I am relieved when I know that some divorcees do not want to cheapen the gift of grace by dismissing the role of performance. I am quite familiar with the reality that some spouses, displeased with the direction of their marital relationship, are looking for an easy way out of a serious commitment. When a spouse gives me flimsy excuses about why the marriage will never work, I cringe in feeling I am being called upon to give my blessing to a poor decision. Common complaints abound that perhaps the partner is a poor communicator, is gone too much, or does not help with family duties. These are real annoyances deserving attention and adjustment, but by themselves they are not necessarily valid reasons to divorce. Having lofty Biblical standards can prevent us from being too loose in our attitude about marital efforts.

Usually when a marriage partner gives weak excuses for seeking a divorce, there is a self-serving agenda pushing the decision along. There is often another man or woman who has captured that person's fancy. Sometimes the divorce decision represents priorities that are greatly imbalanced, as in the case of someone putting career advancement ahead of the marriage commitment. Other times, spouses may seek divorce simply because they are too lazy to apply the effort required to blend the quirks and uniqueness of two differing personalities. Whatever the case, it is possible that some people seek divorce unnecessarily because they refuse to be inconvenienced by the hard work of remaining committed "for better or worse."

Encountering those circumstances, I remind these people that although God indeed offers grace when we fail, He still wants us to do all that can be done to succeed in pursuing His perfect Law. Seeking "cheap grace" is an offense to Him; it represents a thinly veiled attempt to build a life based on self-centered rather than God-centered priorities (there's that pride issue again).

Despite God's realization that we will not meet His standard, He wants us to respect it because He knows it is best for us. He loves us enough to teach excellence and then prod us toward that standard. He is our loving parent who wants us to have right priorities, not because He is trying to torment us with a never-ending list of harsh obligations but because He wants us to have joy in abundance. Following His will is ultimately joy-producing, even if it requires sacrifice along the way.

I am reminded of a man who sat in my office years ago with his wife, to tell her that he had never loved her and though she was a nice person he felt he could never have a good life with her. He wanted out of the marriage so he could find the life of fulfillment he felt he deserved. Giving me no chance to discuss his decision on any deep level, he told his wife good-bye, left my office alone, and filed divorce papers the next day. He professed that he was a Christian, and though he didn't have Biblical grounds he rationalized that God would forgive him and he could still feel safe that God loved him. Of course, his wife was absolutely devastated.

About a year later, this man called my office, asking, "Do you remember me?" Though there was only the one encounter, I had no trouble recalling that earlier conversation, so yes, I remembered him.

"I'm at the very bottom of the barrel, and I need to talk to someone. Can you work me in?" Of course, I did. I was curious to hear what was on his mind. When we met later that day, this man was completely different from the cold, self-assured person I had met the prior year. He was broken and truly humbled. He had tried to live according to his rules, but his new life did not play out as wonderfully as he hoped. He lived a life of self-indulgence, and it produced only emptiness. He had not talked with his wife yet because he knew he had hurt her deeply, but he wondered if I would help him get his life back on track, perhaps even restoring his shattered marriage. I told him I didn't know what we could do about the marriage (that would depend on his wife), but I knew that with God's help he could set his own life right.

In the weeks and months that followed, this man talked about his realization that he had tried to take advantage of God's grace, believing that God was bound by His forgiving nature and could not reject him if he tried life his own way. Indeed, as I assured him that God's forgiveness is vast, he then acknowledged that life outside God's will was a living hell. In time, his former wife joined him in counseling, and they were able to reconcile their marriage (something that happens in less than one out of a hundred cases after the divorce has been finalized). The reconciliation process was neither quick nor easy, and he experienced great agony as he faced the elements in his personality that led to such poor choices. Meanwhile, he learned an invaluable lesson that even as God makes room for human error He also expects us to consult His ways. The price of living outside His laws is steep.

The fourth truth is that *the Law was intended to thwart human arrogance.*

Though not made explicit, there is one overriding message God communicated to the Hebrews as He gave them the Law: "I am the giver of absolutes. It is my prerogative, not yours, to spell out the rules that humanity should follow." Prior to the giving of the Law, God was lenient, giving humans great latitude with free will, and as we have seen it led to disastrous results. Through the Law, God was asserting that there is one necessary ingredient for success in life that they had overlooked, submission to God. In Adam's day, submission was a trait that God required for a holy life; it remains today as a needed characteristic in a life that is pleasing to Him.

When I talk with people, whether privately or at a large conference, about the subject of submission, I find that a fairly high percentage of people recoil at the mere mention of the word. They seem to think, "Oh no; here's one more person who's going to tell me to check my brain at the door and stop thinking for myself." Their defensiveness is then higher than necessary. These folks have yet to understand how submission to God's absolute authority is a far more pleasing way of life than the alternative of self-governance.

Inherent in the requirement of submission is the assumption that humans, left to their own devices, will prove to be untrustworthy. This is why there is a need to surrender human willpower to a higher and more reliable source. It is an unflattering thought, yet true. Left on our own, we do not do a good job of playing God. Arrogance takes over, which causes us to choose priorities that serve self without full regard for potential damage to others.

I have talked with many people who are close to leaving their mate for reasons centered upon a selfish or insensitive agenda. For instance, a husband may be ready to leave his wife because she's not a good housekeeper, or a wife may be ready to abandon her husband because he does not make enough money to buy all that she wants. When I discuss the pros and cons of their decision, I am relieved to have the Word of God on my side as it refers to the disdain that God holds for divorce. "This is not a subject to take lightly," I say. Then I discuss with them why it is so necessary to put the highest priority on maintaining the marriage commitment. I talk about how their submission to God's standard prompts them to explore issues that might otherwise be dismissed if they divorce. For instance, submission causes them to examine more closely their anger management style, fears, insecurities, use of money, communication breakdowns, and defenses.

Without a law teaching submission, humans would have little or no motivation to search for higher truth. "What's in it for me?"

would be the ultimate determinant in any dilemma. God was being good to humans by giving the Law because it is a way to keep personal egos in check. It creates a restraint that causes people to think twice before establishing a self-based set of rules for life.

I want to emphasize the truth that we all have an ongoing need for God's absolutes. That stated, I also acknowledge that humans continue to be quite human until taken into glory by Christ. There are many instances when people place themselves in difficult circumstances, and despite their respect for God's absolutes they illustrate in doing so that they do not possess the ability to live within the parameters of those absolutes. The Law repeatedly exposes the fact that we are simply not righteous. This should be a surprise to no one.

Not too long ago, I spoke with a church leader about a woman who was removed from the church's membership roll because she filed divorce papers against her husband. For years he was physically and verbally abusive toward her and her two children, and finally a school counselor turned him in to the state's child protective services because a son had shown her the many bruises received in a recent beating by this man. (He referred to the beating as a spanking.) After the wife first separated from him, she promised she would not pursue divorce if he would get help and completely cease the abuse. His response was to curse her and the kids. He yelled and cursed at the court-appointed counselor. He refused to follow any procedures to repair the damage to the family. The church membership was fully aware of this woman's plight and most sympathized greatly with her.

When I asked the church leader why she had been removed from church membership, he explained: "We still want her and her kids to come to our church, but not as members. If everyone knows that she filed for divorce without having biblical grounds and without any consequences to that decision, we would be sending a bad message to the rest of the church membership, particularly our younger members." Predictably, the woman chose to take her family elsewhere to church, and they never saw them again.

The Law is most necessary because it gives humans a needed framework for living. But there is one thing that supersedes the Law: love. My approach to people in circumstances of divorce is that I try to be true to the Law so long as I am also true to the loving character of Christ. If following the letter of the Law would result in a judgmental spirit or suspension of common sense, I am willing to examine the path of grace.

It is important for us to keep in mind this perspective about the Law when we examine Jesus' discussion about divorce with the Pharisees as recorded in Matthew 19. Before we explore the Matthew passage, however, let's glean some ideas about Christ's position regarding the Law as recorded in the Sermon on the Mount. As we continue examining the subject of the Law and divorce, then, I would like for us to explore Christ's position regarding the Law. From there we gain some insight into His later words about divorce. We begin there in the next chapter.

Chapter Four

Christ's Impossible Standard and His Enduring Grace

Just to the north of the Sea of Galilee in modern Israel is one of the most serene vistas in all the world. The Mount of the Beatitudes hosts a beautiful chapel surrounded by large shade trees and ornamental gardens. In the springtime, as the land slopes gently down toward the sea, a carpet of yellow flowers brightens the landscape and offers a gorgeous contrast to the fertile farmland just to the west. To the north modest hills and mountains provide the effect of a bowl without cutting off the view to majestic snow-capped Mount Herman in the distance. Clear blue skies prevail on most days, and the breezes off the sea create a feeling of relaxation that makes pilgrims want to linger forever.

My fondness for this peaceful place is accompanied by a worshipful adoration of Christ as I am reminded of the astounding message He spoke on this very spot two thousand years ago. The Sermon on the Mount (recorded in Matthew 5–7) revealed Jesus' mind-set as He planted the seeds for His emerging teachings about grace. Knowing that no other human can come close to fulfilling God's Law, He takes it upon Himself to be the embodiment of one who would satisfy the requirements of the Law, once and for all. In this sermon, He explains exactly what those requirements are—and they are more than the scholars of the Old Testament mandated, as we see in this chapter.

To understand Jesus' teaching about divorce, it is necessary first to comprehend the regard He has for the Mosaic Law. Not only does Jesus hold the Law in high esteem but He raises its already high standard to an even more stringent level. Through this sermon, He communicates that righteousness can be obtained by maintaining the Old Testament laws *plus* a few more requirements that have not been previously mentioned. He teaches that the standard for righteousness is so lofty, so impossible that He is the only one who can attain it.

It is significant that He begins His remarks by pronouncing blessings on the poor in spirit, those who mourn, and those who are meek. By doing so, He is underscoring the notion, "If you are flawed, hurt, or disenfranchised, welcome! You can do business with Me because you are the kind of person that I specialize in." He is showing Himself as radically different from the religious elite who scorned people with problems and imperfections. He is openly stating that He would build His kingdom with people who were needy and aware of their deficiencies. Rather than "Clean up your life and then come to Me," He is saying "Come to Me with all your brokenness. I want you to be one of Mine." The very bedrock of His message was His willingness to work with people who did not make the grade. He refers to these people as the ones who could become the "salt of the earth" and the "light of the world" (Matthew 5:3–16).

This message is just as true today, though many Christians still struggle to find the same inviting spirit that Christ showed toward the hurting and the outcast. I have spoken to many divorcees who are deeply relieved to know that Christ receives them still. He welcomes them despite the broken experiences they have had, both prior to and after their marital breakdown. "Thank you, God," is their cry, "that You would choose to love me in the very midst of my spiritual poverty." Sadly, these same people often report that some fellow believers do not seem as eager to express the message of acceptance or inclusion.

Even though there may be some divorcees who pridefully attempt to abuse God's grace, we must remember that God's ministry to those who cannot measure up to the perfect standard is the core of the gospel. That's what Jesus stood for. As we receive the teachings of the Sermon on the Mount, we dare not ignore the parts where Jesus embraces the broken.

In the Sermon on the Mount, once Jesus indicates His willingness to receive troubled people He explains how His standard for righteousness actually exceeds the standard the Hebrews had known up to that point in time. "Do not think that I came to abolish the Law or the Prophets," he explained. "I did not come to abolish, but to fulfill." Then He discloses His insistence upon complete perfection: "Until heaven and earth pass away, not the smallest letter or stroke shall pass away from the Law until all is accomplished" (Matthew 5:17–18).

Jesus emphasizes: "My kingdom requires that all must be perfect, down to the smallest detail. If you want to be part of that kingdom, the most stringent criteria will be applied to you. I am holy and will accept no blemish, none."

If I were listening to Jesus on the day He spoke these words, I would at this point be confused. In the beginning of His message He spoke words of inclusion to broken, stained persons like me. Right off, I would have felt tremendous relief ("Whew! I like this man. He's talking straight to me. He's telling me that I can be blessed by Him even in my pitiable state."). I would feel warm acceptance as I allowed myself to think that this teacher can love not just religiously correct people but wretches like me as well.

But wait! What's this He's saying? Is He insisting that His kingdom will not come until the Law is fulfilled down to its most minute detail? Just when I thought I had a chance to be a part of His kingdom, its salt and light, I am hearing that He requires total perfection. What's the deal? His words seem contradictory. My confusion would stem from the fact that I do not understand that Jesus is laying the groundwork for His doctrine of grace. His message at this point is not finished.

In the next paragraphs, we explore some of the "for instances" that Jesus gives regarding His perfect standard for righteousness. As we do, let's keep in mind that the examples He gives *were leading His listeners toward the doctrine of grace*. Many people take His words as hard instructions for what believers must or must not do in order to be received by God as righteous. In a sense, this is correct because Jesus requires perfection. But to hold individuals to His perfect standard misses the entire point of His incarnation. The forthcoming message is: "I'm going to explain to you My extremely high standard for righteousness to make the point that true righteousness is out of your human reach. The good news is this. As you see Me live out this standard to its utmost detail, I will allow you to claim My righteousness as your own. No, you can never be perfect, but as you realize this, you'll be relieved to know that I will become your perfection!"

Let me pause here to clarify that my thoughts are influenced by Paul's discussion of the Law in his letter to the Romans. He is entirely clear in his introductory chapters as he expounds on the doctrine of sin—that we are each deeply infected by imperfection, to such an extent that we seem to be irreparably separated from God. His well-known words state that "all have sinned and fall short of the glory of God" (Romans 3:23). Then he specifically points out that "the Law came in that the transgression might increase" (Romans 5:20a). That is, the Law shows us what the perfectly righteous life is; in doing so, it exposes the harsh reality that no one is close to meeting that standard. Rather than remaining as a matter of prosecution and accusation, though, our understanding of the Law leads us toward the doctrine of grace. "But where sin increased, grace abounded all the more" (Romans 5:20b). That is, the more aware we are of the insidious nature of sin, the more profound the love of God appears.

Paul also states that we were "made to die to the Law" (Romans 7:4). Why is this? Is it because the Law is not good? Not at all. The Law is perfect, but because we are not, we cannot be "wed" to the Law. We are to die to the Law so that we can be wed to something different: the grace of Christ. By stating that we must die to the Law, Paul does not disregard the Law. "May it never be" is his reply to that thought, as expressed in Romans 6:2. He reveres God's standard for perfection, and he anguishes at the reality of his inability to live in it ("Wretched man that I am," he calls himself in Romans 7:24).

In the same way, let us hold Jesus' teaching of perfection in awe, not seeing Him as excusing us from considering God's standards but exposing us as the inadequate people that we are.

The For Instances

When Jesus spoke in His Sermon on the Mount, He was underscoring just how out of reach the Law really is. In a sense, He was showing how each of us is under certain judgment because we are so inadequate in our ability to live within its standards. But even as He exposes our frailty, He is laying the foundation for grace that can be found in Him. This does not invite us to interpret His words in a way that allows us to take the Law loosely, causing us then to misuse His gift of grace. Rather, we can interpret His words with a heart of gratitude despite our inabilities; He will take us by the hand to the Father. No matter how grossly we fall short, He (not the Law) will be our sufficiency.

Once Jesus explains that His standard of righteousness has to be fulfilled to "the smallest stroke or letter," He then gives several examples of what He means. He makes no secret regarding the truth that God requires total perfection before righteousness can be declared. In each, He mentions the Mosaic Law, followed by His new, more difficult standard. Let's examine three of these examples and use them as a bridge to help us understand His later words about divorce, recorded in Matthew 19.

Thoughts of Anger

Jesus explains to His audience, "You have been told, 'You shall not commit murder' . . . but I say to you that everyone who is angry against his brother shall be deemed guilty" (Matthew 5:21–22). Until then, the Jewish people thought along the lines of "If I have never been guilty of killing someone, that shows I am a righteous person; God will be pleased with me." Certainly a high percentage of Jesus' audience would be able to lay claim to righteousness on the basis of that criterion.

Jesus, however, is saying, "My standard for righteousness goes well beyond what you have been taught. You see, I cannot pronounce anyone righteous who has ever had inappropriately angry thoughts against another person. Not only do I require that your outer deeds conform to perfection, but your innermost thoughts must also be pure. You should not entertain one hateful thought."

Surely this pronouncement caught his listeners off guard. They must have been reminded of numerous instances when they had harbored resentment, felt bitterness, or looked scornfully upon another's weakness. Not one person in His audience could step forward and confidently state, "I've never harbored inappropriate anger—not once." Instead, each person must have realized immediately that Jesus was placing the bar way too high.

The same is true for us today. We know from other biblical teachings that there are moments when anger can be consistent with a discerning life. For instance, Ephesians 4:26 allows anger but without sin. We know that Jesus communicated from a position of righteous anger on several occasions when He witnessed callous disregard for godliness. We also know, though, that there is a form of anger (this is what Jesus was referring to in the sermon) that is not at all righteous. Each of us is prone to this unhealthy anger at some time or another. For instance, Ephesians 4:31 instructs us to stay away from such forms of anger as bitterness, wrath, clamor, slander, and malice. As harmful anger is indulged, it keeps us from knowing and experiencing God's love. Regrettably, whether recently or in the distant past, we all recall moments when we embodied such unflattering traits.

Suppose that at this point in His sermon Jesus asks the question, "How many of you could say that you have never been inappropriately angry?" No one is able to raise a hand, claiming such perfection. His goal is to show that no one is inwardly pure, and surely this first example makes His point.

Thoughts of Lust

Next, Jesus picks a theme that proves even more humbling to His listeners. He says, "You have heard that you are never to commit adultery, but I say to you that if you lustfully look upon another woman you're just as guilty as if you had committed adultery" (Matthew 5:27–28).

If the teaching about anger caused the people to pause for serious personal reflection, this teaching penetrates even deeper. Jesus becomes intensely personal as He asks them to be starkly honest about their inner-thought world. "Perhaps you'd like to think of yourself as righteous for never committing adultery," is His insinuation. Surely a high percentage of His listeners can say that indeed they have not been unfaithful in their marriage, so until now they have presumed that they can take pride in their virtue. But now, Jesus is intensifying the dilemma: "In my kingdom, you cannot be deemed righteous if you have had one single lustful thought for another person. Not one stray thought."

Once again, the listeners certainly feel disqualified as they think, "Well, just as the anger criteria did, I guess this puts me outside the realm of complete purity. I hate to admit it, but I've had plenty of moments when stray sexual thoughts have crossed my mind. Sometimes I've dwelt too long on curiosities about sex. There's no way I can claim innocence here."

Through the years I have spoken with countless men and women about their emotional and relationship problems. As a therapist, I have heard virtually every story imaginable. But if there is one area where people are most prone to close themselves off from me, it is sexuality. Understandably so. God intends sex to be an intensely private matter between a husband and wife. It does not need to be broadly discussed with others, particularly among people who might turn personal disclosure into gossip. But even in a relationship where it is safe and acceptable to reveal sexual concerns, people do not speak freely because of the potential of revealing damaging facts about themselves. No one likes to admit it, but everyone can let sexual fantasies gain a stronghold or at least harbor thoughts contrary to sexual purity—even if only for a fleeting moment.

In a study by Christian psychologist Archibald Hart, six hundred evangelical Christian men were surveyed to determine how frequently they thought about sex. Approximately 80 percent acknowledged thinking about it daily or more than daily. None acknowledged never thinking about sex. (The entire study is detailed in his book *The*

Sexual Man.) Simply put, Christians have sexual thoughts. Though other studies have shown that strong Christians may be less inclined than the average person to act out inappropriately on those impulses, none of us is immune.

Jesus clearly looks beyond mere outward behavior and peers directly into our innermost thoughts and desires. In each case, He finds every individual lacking, whether married or divorced. "Don't think that you can impress God with a clean-looking exterior," He implies, "when you have errant, sinful thoughts lurking below. I'm aware of all that is in you, and I have discerned that no one passes the test of righteousness, as determined by my criteria."

In emphasizing the interior of each individual, Jesus is leveling the playing field. No one can claim spiritual superiority, even if it seems he or she has all the right lifestyle ingredients in place. That being the case, there is no need for any person to think of himself or herself as above others, just as there is no need for anyone to assume lower status. Jesus wants to take His listeners (and us, His readers) to a place of humility so we become more receptive to the message that each person needs a Righteous Substitute to plead their case before God.

The Problem of Divorce

As Jesus continues giving examples of how His standard for righteousness compares to the standard of Mosaic Law, He addresses the subject of divorce. "In days past," He explains, "you have been allowed to divorce your wife as long as you write it up in an appropriate document. But I say to you that if you divorce your wife, except in the case of adultery, you cause her to become an adulteress if she remarries. The same is true if you marry a woman who has been divorced. That marriage would constitute an act of adultery as well" (Matthew 5:31–32).

This is one of the major passages that cause anxiety in divorcees who want to remarry. Not wanting to remain isolated for the rest of their lives, many would like to become joined in a new, vibrant marriage. When they choose to do so, unless adultery was a part of the marital dissolution, they know they are counter to God's best. Let's be careful, as we consider this passage, not to be so black-and-white that we become judgmental. In one sense, Jesus *is* being black-and-white; yet, we are wisest to read with the realization that at the same time He is teaching a whole new way of thinking about righteousness.

First, let's acknowledge that the Jewish people of Jesus' day had something of a contradictory approach to marriage and divorce. On the positive side, marriage was generally held in high regard and family cohesion was strong. In their biblical teaching they were told that God is not at all in favor of divorce. "I hate divorce" was the opinion rendered by God, as recorded in Malachi 2:16. They knew that God wanted them to hold the marriage commitment in highest regard, and most people of that day did so. On the other hand, divorce was an extremely simple procedure, and it did not necessarily require awful events in order to pursue it. The woman of that day, in the eyes of the Law, was regarded as just barely above a possession, and she was at the absolute disposal of either her husband or her father. Some Jews insisted that a woman could only be divorced if she had committed sexual indecency. Others determined that a woman could be divorced if she was a poor housekeeper, if she was quarrelsome, or if she was too friendly toward other men. The opinions about divorce ranged from one extreme to the other, so Jesus used His sermon to explain where He came down on the matter.

Jesus let it be known that He always appealed to perfect principles when discussing the subject of righteousness. His standard allowed no divorce at all, none. (We see this even more clearly in the next chapter as we examine His remarks in Matthew 19.) Jesus stood for 100 percent purity, through and through. He wanted no one at any time to be divorced.

Here is what Jesus was saying, which should help you understand this lofty ideal concerning marriage and divorce: "I do not want anyone ever to be divorced. Marriage is a way of protecting sexual purity, one man being sexually committed to one woman, and that's it. So if a man divorces his wife and she then marries someone else, she has slept with two men—meaning, she's not living according to My perfect standard of sexual purity. On the purest level, we'd have to call that adultery. Now, if she has already committed adultery prior to the divorce, then the remarriage doesn't make her an adulteress because she has already become one."

Divorcees often become caught in troubled emotions because their dissolved marriage puts them in a position of breaking Christ's perfect standard if they decide to date and remarry. Naturally they question, "Does this mean that I'll forevermore be labeled as an adulterer?" In the strictest sense, Jesus is stating that unless the former spouse committed adultery, the sexual activity in a remarriage is considered outside God's perfect plan, given the fact that God's intent is for a husband and wife to remain married with no exception.

I remind divorcees that as Jesus gives this stringent teaching, He is not communicating with a heart of condemnation. He is speaking specifically about the standard of complete perfection that holiness requires. As a benign exception, He recognizes that when a spouse has committed adultery it changes the rules for the offended spouse, and a resulting divorce and remarriage are granted for the purpose of finding a fresh start. When divorcees remarry, even though the marriage does not originate from the act of adultery, they do not have to do so with lasting shame for failing to measure up to the perfect standard. God's grace is intact. They need to be mindful that though remarriage is not God's first choice, they should become all the more committed to pursuing remarriage with an increased willingness to let Him guide the relationship.

Divorce and remarriage are not consistent with Jesus' perfect standard for righteousness, just as lustful thoughts or inappropriate anger are not. In His Sermon on the Mount, Jesus' major goal is to communicate that the only person who can be considered righteous is someone who has absolutely zero flaws—no misguided anger, no lustful thoughts, no divorce. As His ministry continued to unfold, He wanted His followers to discover that He would be the only one to maintain those requirements. Here, He is *not* burdening His listeners with a harsh attitude of rejection, saying "I'll bless you only if you never lust, never get angry, or never divorce." Such a mind-set would ensure a one-man kingdom consisting of no one beyond Himself. Rather, in establishing such stringent standards He is laying the groundwork for grace because He knows that as His ministry expands, His followers will learn that there is much more to the story. He loves individuals so much that He will pay the penalty for their inability to live perfectly, and as the consummate substitute He will present any believer to God as one who is clothed in His perfect righteousness. Those in His audience who are poor in spirit, mournful, and meek can still find hope because His death will complete the punishment phase for the breaking of the Law.

Because we explore further His "adultery clause" in the next chapter, I'd like to pause at this point and summarize some key elements in His Sermon teaching.

"Lawbreakers" Welcome Here

Until this encounter with Christ, the average Hebrew citizen had a large load of insecurity to carry regarding the subject of acceptance by God. Approaching God hinged entirely upon maintaining absolutely correct performance of ritual and strict adherence to the mandates of the Mosaic Law. Many Christians today feel similarly that they can remain in God's good graces only as long as they keep the Law, usually as it is decreed by a strong-willed authority figure.

One pastor, whom we'll refer to as Max, was proud of the fact that he kept a close watch over the people God brought into his congregation. "After visiting our church for a few weeks, people will ask if they can join the church. Almost always I'll ask them to wait another month or two to see if they are really serious about being involved. Because I believe that a church should encourage its members to be active participants in its programs, it would be irresponsible to let someone join with the idea that it's OK just to be a passive, in-and-out type of member." Max had strong principles, a trait worthy of admiration.

Whenever a situation arose where a couple in his church was separating or divorcing, Max maintained this same principled mind-set as he took an activist role in approaching the problem. One woman, whom we'll call Brenda, described how this approach worked with her: "My husband has been an extremely difficult man to live with. We've been married eight years, and he's held a job for about two of those years. He could get a decent job, but he just doesn't want to work. I make a decent salary with my job, but we just barely cover the bills each month. Our five-year-old son goes to a private babysitter, meaning my husband has plenty of time to get a job. But he doesn't! Sometimes he'll play golf, but a lot of his time he just stays at home. He may do yard work, but more often than not he's piddling on the computer. He says he wants to be a writer (he loves music), but so far he's done nothing except buy some music software packages. He doesn't talk with me much when I'm home. He's not a very good dad because he says he's not patient with our son. We virtually never have sex and we have no social life, except for times when my son and I visit my sister's family."

Max sympathized with Brenda's plight. He had even conversed several times with her husband about a husband's leadership role. But the husband remained stubbornly entrenched in his pattern of laziness and detachment and showed no signs of wanting to change. When Brenda told Max that she had asked her husband to move out, Max hit the roof. "The integrity of marriage must be preserved!" he said. "I certainly hope this is not the first step toward divorce." Though she knew it was against her pastor's desire, Brenda explained that she had told her husband that if he had no intentions of being an engaged husband and an employed provider, she would no longer enable his laziness. Brenda explained to Max that she would no longer participate in such nonsense.

Sure enough, as the months passed the husband made no attempt to talk with Brenda about their marriage. He still didn't look for a job. He saw their son only occasionally and often didn't even show up for time with him. So Brenda filed for and received a divorce.

Shortly after the divorce was finalized, Brenda received a letter from Max. In it he explained that she could hold no committee positions and she would have to cease teaching in the preschool choir program. She would be allowed to keep her membership, but until she reconciled with her husband she could not participate in leadership.

Brenda called Max and told him not to worry about her being a poor influence to the people in his church; she would go to another one. Max told some other church members: "If we're going to call ourselves a church that loves God, we've got to be serious about living right. Unfortunately, that may cause some folks to move on down the road."

Is this the mind-set Jesus wants to instill in His followers as He explains His perfect principles? Max thought so. In fact, he often referred to a summary statement that Jesus makes in the Sermon on the Mount: "Be perfect, just as your Father in heaven is perfect" (Matthew 5:48).

When Jesus says "Be perfect," He is summarizing what must be done in order to commune fully with God. *The rest of His message is* "I will be that perfection for you, since it is so far beyond your capacity." The entire message of Christ's redemptive work is predicated on the realization that no one, despite the finest efforts, can attain perfection. He wants people who have failed in many areas of life, even in marriage, to come to Him. If He could put a sign on the front of the entry gates to His kingdom, it would boldly proclaim, "SINNERS WELCOME HERE."

People like Max, who withdraw fellowship and nurturance from someone like Brenda, say in effect, "We welcome the righteous here, but if you prove to be flawed, we'll have to reconsider the welcome." Though Max would say that he did not withdraw fellowship—only the privilege to teach and serve on committees—the net effect was that she never fellowshipped with his congregation again. This is virtually always the case for people like Brenda.

You might ask, "Did Brenda make the right decision in eventually divorcing her husband?" There is no easy answer to the question. Frankly, I cannot state one way or the other if it was the correct determination. Clearly the husband showed little or no regard for biblical instructions regarding how a husband should love his wife. He had very little interest in sex. (Was he gay? Brenda and some of her friends strongly suspected there might be some leanings in that direction, which might explain his extreme passivity.) What picture of marriage was being presented to their son, and how would it affect him? Brenda had no simple task in front of her as she tried to determine the best path to take. My advice to her would be to consult the Lord mightily and live according to the directives He gave her. Risky advice? Maybe . . . yet I understand that it is not my job to be her Holy Spirit.

Illumination, Not Condemnation

Many people use the perfect principles expressed by Jesus to determine if they can accept or reject other people. It would be safe to say that Jesus did not intend to pronounce absolute truth for the purpose of separating acceptable people from the unacceptable. His teachings were absolute in the sense that they were irrefutably correct. He was not, however, establishing norms whereby guilty sinners could judge one another. Some performance-minded Christians insist, "But if it's in the Bible, we've got to exhort people to be faithful to its truth." My response to this sentiment is, "It is noble that you want to remain true to Jesus' words, but let's be careful to maintain a commitment to His truths while also maintaining a commitment to His grace." Sometimes, people act as if the possession of good knowledge makes it permissible to create a pecking order within a group—a practice not encouraged in any biblical teaching.

Jesus' words in the Sermon on the Mount are meant to be an illuminating description of God's perfect character that shows humanity's flawed character to be a less-than-sufficient means of attaining righteousness. Certainly these words also set goals we should strive to meet, and they are meant ultimately to edify followers of Christ. They are not meant, however, to become a foundation for judgment or rejection.

I spoke once with a first grade teacher who described how she sometimes had to train her children how to receive her words of instruction or correction. For instance, this teacher had a boy in her class who had a strong desire to please her and do things right. He came from a solid family that had instilled in him a respect for those in authority. On one particular assignment, the boy did not follow the instructions, so the teacher knelt with the boy at his desk and corrected his mistakes. The boy was fighting hard to hold back tears. When the teacher asked what he was thinking, he blurted out, "I feel so bad when I can't do what you tell me I'm supposed to do!" She realized he did not yet understand a fundamental element within her character. As his teacher, she gave him instructions regarding the way things should be done, but she could still accept him as a person if he failed to follow her instructions.

Some people leave little room for failure. They examine the principles of the Bible, and then they make it their job to evaluate who conforms and who does not. Those who don't conform can be censured and devalued. Like the compassionate first grade teacher, Christ is (thankfully) not so severe. His principles serve as illuminations, showing the way toward godliness, yet He spares us from condemnation when we fall short. In explaining His mission to Nicodemus, Jesus says, "For God did not send the Son into the world to condemn the world, but that the world through Him might be saved" (John 3:17). Later the apostle Paul echoes the same theme: "There is therefore now no condemnation for those who are in Christ Jesus" (Romans 8:1).

In my counseling practice and in seminars, I often talk with people about lofty principles. For instance, here is one common principle: do not let other people determine the traits that guide you in your relationships. Rather than being a reactor, be an initiator, and filter your lifestyle choices through God's design for your life. I teach that you can maintain firmness in your decisions even when others are contrary and difficult. It is sound advice, I believe, and it leads to good results when applied. Yet I can honestly state that not one single person I have advised in this way has followed my instructions to perfection. Nonetheless, I continue to teach healthy principles. There is always room for growth; we all just have to keep working on it.

Something is wrong in Christian circles when we use God's perfect principles to explain or justify why a fellow sinner (such as a divorcee) should receive condemnation, rejection, or devaluation. Yes, if a Christian has a life pattern of perpetually snubbing godliness or is habitually manipulative and devious in deliberately disobeying God, we may have reason to confront or discipline. Sometimes we may even decide to separate ourselves from that person if it is clear that the wrongdoer shows no sign of repentance or remorse. That stated, we can also recognize that a high percentage of Christians who have failed feel great regret for not measuring up to the perfect biblical standard. Far from being crass manipulators of Christian principles, most feel dejected. They wish to be more capable of maintaining the highest standard and may have failed after enormous struggle or through no fault of their own. These people do not need judgment, but encouragement and understanding and compassion.

In fact, while speaking in the Sermon on the Mount, to clarify His perfect standards Christ recognizes that humans tend to keep score on others' behavior. He pointedly addresses the potential for people to condemn one another by stating: "Do not judge lest you be judged. For in the way you judge you will be judged; and by your standard of measure it will be measured to you. And why do you look at the speck that is in your brother's eye but do not notice the log that is in your own eye?" (Matthew 7:1–3). After declaring what must be done to attain perfection, Jesus clearly warns that no human is immune from frailty, and no human is entitled to scorn another's imperfection.

Since divorce is clearly an instance of imperfection, of failure, it is important to take a similarly nonjudgmental stance toward those who divorce. This is not to say, as I've pointed out in earlier chapters, that Christians should not hold strongly to a firm standard of marriage. We certainly should. Let's seriously receive Christ's challenge to perfection even as we determine how to love and minister to those among us who fall short. This balance is critical within the fellowship of believers.

In the next chapter, we examine Jesus' words about divorce as recorded in Matthew 19. They are an extension of what He has said in the Sermon on the Mount, and they are also an extension of what God spoke to Adam in mankind's first set of instructions.

Chapter Five

The Perfect Principle

Being correct can be a dangerous thing. I am reminded of a man in my counseling office who succinctly summarized his relationship problems by admitting, "I'm so right, I'm wrong." He went on to explain that his sense of correctness prompted him to be easily critical, impatient, and bossy. Can you relate?

The Pharisees of Jesus' time could certainly relate. The Pharisaic movement was founded on a desire to show respect for God by keeping His Law down to its finest detail. Realizing that many Jews were lax in paying homage to the Lord, they committed their lives as a living example of piety and devotion. Nothing wrong with that!

The problem with the Pharisees was not in their stated intent, but in the result of their good intentions. As they sought to live correctly before God, they could not help but notice that others barely thought about God's desires at all. Likewise, they surely recognized that some people paid lip service to godliness yet were not willing to give all of themselves to the Lord. They were also frustrated and concerned because they were uncomfortable at the thought of people trivializing God.

In today's evangelical churches, we likewise have individuals who take it upon themselves to study the Word of God carefully so they can then live it correctly. They hope to preserve godly character in a world that otherwise might just wink at God while going along in its own self-absorbed patterns. Not only is it *not* wrong to do so, it is good and necessary. Christians are called to be holy (separate), and we can find delight in knowing that we are committed to a way of life pleasing to God, distinct from the improprieties of secular thinking. As was the case of the Pharisees, though, it is possible to be so committed to correctness that the result is a critical nature, a feeling of superiority, and a condemning spirit.

A common ingredient of this overly correct mind-set is insecurity. Most people excessively devoted to correctness fail to recognize their insecurity; they scoff at anyone who might suggest such a notion. Nonetheless, it is there. Perhaps the easiest way to detect this underlying insecurity is in the extent to which they are threatened by one who openly shows disdain for their way of thinking. They respond with defensiveness and try to invalidate the one who is different.

When Jesus burst onto the scene with His astonishing miracles, His grace-focused teaching, and His compassion for the religiously incorrect, the Pharisees in their insecurity took it upon themselves to invalidate Him at every opportunity. They were offended that He would dare enter their realm, and act as if He had insights from God that differed from theirs. They sought to expose Him as the fraud and heretic they believed He surely was. Whereas a secure group of people would be more willing to at least consider a differing perspective, they could not bring themselves to do so. Their only goal was to discredit Jesus and protect themselves.

The Pharisees brought this offensive mind-set to their confrontation with Jesus about the subject of divorce, as recorded in Matthew 19:3–9. By this time, Jesus was enjoying immense popularity; these men were feverishly looking for ways to show themselves to be more learned. To elevate themselves, they had to bring Him down. Rather than taking the front-door approach, which might have meant direct confrontation or debate, their favorite tactic was to ask sly questions. They hoped He would answer in ways that would pit Jesus against the common wisdom of the day, thereby making Him look foolish. Of course, Jesus saw through their approach and proved to be far wiser than they imagined. He would not be caught in their snare.

When the Pharisees asked Jesus about His opinion on divorce (Matthew 19:3), they were aware that this was a thorny issue because so many opinions existed. For instance, it was common thinking of the day that a man could divorce his wife if he found some indecency in her. The controversy was over how to interpret *indecency*. Some believed it meant adultery and nothing else. A woman might be incredibly difficult to live with, but as long as she remained sexually faithful no divorce could be sought. At the other extreme, some believed that indecency could include a wife spoiling her husband's meat, appearing in public with unbound hair, or speaking disrespectfully about her husband's parents. Some believed a man could divorce his wife for reasons of desertion or insanity; others taught that these were not just causes. (There is no indication that women could initiate divorce in those days. It was a male-dominated culture.)

The Pharisees must have been almost giddy as they reasoned, "Let's ask Jesus His beliefs about divorce. Because there are so many opinions on this subject, His answer will surely offend lots of people." They had no real concern about His position on the matter; they only used this opportunity as a vehicle to make Him look foolish.

Here's how the scriptures report this exchange: "And some Pharisees came to Him, testing Him and saying, 'Is it lawful for a man to divorce his wife for any cause at all?' And He answered and said, 'Have you not read, that He who created them from the beginning made them male and female, and said, "For this cause a man shall leave his father and mother and shall cleave to his wife, and the two shall become one flesh"? Consequently, they are no longer two, but one flesh. What therefore God has joined together, let no man separate'" (Matthew 19:3–6).

In this first of two stages of questioning, the Pharisees simply posed the general question about divorce ("Jesus, tell us your belief"). They hoped that such an open-ended question would provide Him enough rope that He would hang Himself with a controversial response. Jesus, though, proved to be far more skilled in His answer than they anticipated. Rather than committing to a less-than-perfect position, He referred to perfect principles.

In essence, through this response He was saying: "You folks want to pull Me into your present-day debate about the technicalities of divorce, but I'll have none of that. My standard for a God-pleasing marriage is total perfection. Let's go back to the beginning and look at God's plan for marriage as it was established prior to sin's entrance into the world. God intended for a husband to love his wife in such a unique way that it would be like no other relationship. His original design for marriage was a relationship so good, so beautiful, that it could always be held as the standard. So rather than ask Me about divorce, let's focus on the fact that God never intended anyone to be divorced, ever. Whenever I speak on the subject of marriage, this is the standard I will point people toward."

This displeased His Pharisaic questioners because Jesus actually showed Himself to be more appropriately concerned with God's standards of righteousness than they were. "Wow! This guy is clever," they must have reasoned. "We can't let Him one-up us like this. We must maneuver Him to commit to a position on divorce." So they narrowed the focus of their question and tried again. Matthew 9:7 states, "They said to Him, 'Why then did Moses command to give her a certificate of divorce and send her away?'" Quoting from Deuteronomy 24:1–4, they were hoping to get Jesus away from His comments about the perfection that existed prior to sin. They wanted Him to focus instead on the state of marriage after sin had prompted the need for the Law.

Briefly, Jesus commented on the Mosaic Law. Verse 8 states: "He said to them, 'Because of your hardness of heart, Moses permitted you to divorce your wives.'" Thus Jesus acknowledged that divorce was permissible under the Law, but He did not comment at this point about the legal grounds for it (as the Pharisees hoped He would).

Keep in mind that when Moses gave the original law of divorce, he was issuing the words given to him by God. Clarifying this pronouncement, Jesus explained that God (through Moses) allowed divorce because there were some instances where spouses were so hardened in attitude that a reasonable marital life could not proceed. In this respect, Jesus gave an answer to their question about the motives behind divorce. People can sometimes be so stubborn, so entrenched in ungodly ways of living that they refuse to bend, or they refuse to live with the mind of love that is essential for a thriving relationship. It is an unflattering truth, but hardened hearts, according to Jesus, cause divorce. He was not saying that He liked the idea of divorce; rather, He was acknowledging the prideful, painful state of mind that leads to a broken marriage.

Once He commented on the Mosaic Law, Jesus took up again the theme that the Pharisees had tried to sidestep: "But from the beginning it has not been this way." Rather than getting bogged down in their insistence that He should wrangle over legalisms, Jesus was insisting, "Let's go back and look at the perfect principle." He then elaborated about the purest approach to marriage, and in doing so He repeated words similar to those in the Sermon on the Mount. Verse 9 reads "And I say to you, whoever divorces his wife, except for immorality, and marries another woman commits adultery."

In His conversation with the Pharisees, Jesus was indicating that He wanted nothing to do with their legalistic nitpicking. Jesus was upholding the concept of sexual purity. Only when sex is experienced within a monogamous, marital relationship can it be completely pure. When a man sets his wife aside and chooses to marry another woman, that falls short of the perfect principle of sexual purity.

Any divorce is considered to be a shortfall of God's perfect principle, just as any remarriage is. The marriage relationship was intended from the beginning to be an experiential picture of God's unadulterated love for His own, so Jesus was emphasizing to the Pharisees: "Rather than focusing on how you can get out of a marriage, focus on the fact that God never wanted any divorce at all. Focus only on what is most pure."

The clause "except for immorality" was an aside made in the context of Jesus' teaching that a second marriage can be technically referred to as adulterous. "Any time you choose to discard one wife in order to move on to another," His reasoning went, "you are falling short of the standard of sexual purity. If, however, your wife has already committed adultery, you would not be held responsible for that broken standard of sexual purity." Jesus was clarifying His statement about who would be considered responsible for breaking the perfect standard.

Today, some people point to this exception clause and claim, "If you fail to meet the criteria established by Jesus, you are using poor judgment and you are living outside the will of God." This reasoning can create considerable tension for people who divorce without adultery being the reason for the marital demise. They often question, "Will God's blessing be removed from my life since my decision does not match Jesus' pronouncement?"

As individuals try to come to terms with Jesus' position about divorce, great care is to be used in the manner it is received. First, I begin with the presumption that Jesus meant what He said: adultery is the clearest indicator that divorce is a viable option. If the beauty of the sexual union between husband and wife is violated, an adulterer has effectively bonded to two mates, an irreconcilable condition that was never intended by God. Nevertheless, in Jesus' appeal to the perfect standard He indicated that He had compassion for those whose marriage was torn apart by infidelity.

How are we to respond, though, to divorcees who could not cite adultery as the cause of the marital failure? My response is to treat them in the same fashion I would treat anyone who fell short of all the other standards of scripture. I will love them. Even as we would want them to factor Christ's perfect standards into their decision-making process, we can be clear in letting them know that they can still find grace. I want to maintain respect for Christ's teaching while also maintaining respect for His character. Jesus was clear and open regarding His beliefs about right and wrong, and He was equally clear regarding His willingness to love those who fell short.

Let's take a difficult illustration to underscore the necessity of a graceful mind-set. A woman we'll call Terri was in dire straits because her husband, whom we'll call Jack, left her and her two children. In their ten years of marriage there were approximately as many as thirty incidents of physical abuse. She suffered broken ribs and many bruises. He was persistently mean to their seven- and five-year-old children and often beat them far beyond mere spankings. Verbal abuse, with cursing, name calling, and threats, occurred almost weekly for years. Jack once hit his wife while she was four months pregnant, causing her to fall on her stomach. As a direct result, Terri lost the baby; Jack showed no remorse.

Terri had tried on numerous occasions to establish boundaries, though her efforts fell short because she felt emotionally weak and trapped because she had no way to make a living while caring for two young children. Finally she told him that his behavior would not be tolerated anymore and that she wanted him to leave the home. When Jack left, he closed the joint checking account and cleaned out the savings account. He left no indication of a new address. He paid no bills and provided no means of support. Having been a stay-at-home mom from the time of their first child's birth, Terri was in a major bind. She had no job, and awful memories of a husband who was a wife and child abuser; now she had no way of paying the house mortgage and utility bills, or of buying groceries.

When Terri consulted a lawyer about how she might gain access to their money, the lawyer explained that the courts could not intervene on her behalf unless a divorce was in progress. By now she knew Jack had no intention of fulfilling his obligations. Their marriage was not repairable. They had been briefly separated several times, but this time there was a definite sense of finality. Finally Terri instructed her lawyer to draw up the necessary legal documents, and to set up a temporary hearing with the courts so that her financial needs could be addressed. When Jack was served the documents at his office, he called Terri and once again went into a rage. He told her to keep her eyes open at all times because he'd like nothing more than to slit her throat.

All during the marriage, Jack claimed to be a Christian. In fact, he had attended a Bible college years earlier. When several friends and family members heard of their marital problems through the years, they talked with him about going to counseling and looking into the possibility of medical treatment for his mood swings. He would agree that was a good idea yet never follow through on the advice. Ultimately, Jack would submit to no instruction or accountability.

What would Jesus tell Terri if she asked Him about the desperate nature of her circumstances? Would He say, "I realize you have an extremely negative situation, and if he had sexual relations with another woman I'd tell you that you are free to divorce. But until that happens, you'll have to remain married"? Would he say, "You are free to separate, but you'll have to let him be the one to file the divorce papers. In the meantime, if he keeps all the money and lets your electricity get cut off and offers no help for the groceries, you'll have to fend for yourself as best you can"?

Of course, we don't know exactly what Jesus would say; nor is the Bible instructive in this particular situation. So we have to interpret His principles as intelligently as we can. Mandating that she should wait until Jack had sexual relations with another woman would only subject her to more abuse. Terri was in a sick, destructive relationship and needed to get away for her own safety and that of her children. Are we being less than Christian to admit this and love her through such an ordeal?

Matthew 18:15–17 gives another of Jesus' teachings, this time about confronting a Christian brother who persists in a pattern of sin. It specifies that one should confront a person with the hope of restoring him or her to truth. If that fails, one or two more should confront him again. If that fails, the issue of discipline is to be taken to the larger church body. If that fails, he or she should be removed. This is harsh, but Jesus realized that sometimes people can be impervious to reason; sadly, there are times when the only thing that can solve the ongoing problem is to permanently sever ties.

Does this teaching apply to all relationships except marriage? Are we to allow aberrant behavior in home life? Questions like these muddy the waters and illustrate how awkward our decision making can be if we make no allowance for grace. I can honestly say that I do not know how Jesus would advise Terri, but I am certain that He would love her regardless of the decision she made.

In the Matthew 19 passage, Jesus renders His teaching about the ideal standard for marriage and divorce; at the same time, He is sidestepping the Pharisees' invitation to become a participant in haggling over legalisms. Even as He speaks quite firmly regarding His belief about divorce, His heart is distinctly different from His inquisitors'. Today, when Christians speak with one another about biblical ideals, they communicate with incompleteness as they appeal to perfect principles yet are unable to show grace if the principle is not met. A delicate balance is needed purporting to speak on Christ's behalf. Rather than confronting divorcees only with questions regarding the correctness of their decision, we represent Christ most fully when we see them as people in pain who need the loving reassurance that they can still count on Christian brothers and sisters to pray on their behalf and to provide encouragement while they discern God's call upon their lives.

Paul's Commonsense Teaching

If there was one person in the early New Testament church who wanted to aggressively distance himself from a judgmental mind-set, it was the apostle Paul, who was trained in the strict standards of the Pharisaic tradition. Paul came to understand that the Law was not at all a means to righteousness, but a means to illustrate how desperately we each need a Savior who will perfectly represent us before God. Paul consistently teaches that rigidity only damages the spiritual vitality of the church.

Just as a harsh interpretation of Christ's words represents a miscalculation of His core message, so is it also erroneous to interpret Paul's teachings outside the mind of grace. Paul did not comment on the subjects of divorce and marriage with the intention of bringing judgment to those who fall short. To think that he did so indicates a serious misunderstanding of his consistent disdain for a rejecting spirit. Rather, in the tradition of Jesus, he spoke in terms of perfect principles, pointing people toward the best way to find fullness in the Christian walk.

Paul's comments in I Corinthians 7 are often cited as one of the two biblically acceptable reasons for divorce. He referred to the possibility of non-Christian spouses leaving their Christian mates, stating that if they actually leave the Christian is not under bondage. That is, he or she is free to pursue legal divorce because of the spouse's desertion:

> But to the married I give instructions, not I, but the Lord, that the wife should not leave her husband (but if she does leave, let her remain unmarried, or else be reconciled to her husband), and that the husband should not send his wife away. But to the rest I say, not the Lord, that if any brother has a wife who is an unbeliever, and she consents to live with him, let him not send her away. And a woman who has an unbelieving husband, and he consents to live with her, let her not send her husband away. For the unbelieving husband is sanctified by his wife, and the unbelieving wife is sanctified through her believing husband; for otherwise your children are unclean, but now they are holy. Yet if the unbelieving one leaves, let him leave; the brother or the sister is not under bondage in such cases, but God has called us to peace [I Corinthians 7:10–15].

There were at least twenty-five years between the ministry of Jesus and Paul's writing of the first Corinthian letter. As the body of believers grew, Christians were curious to understand how to apply Christ's teachings in their daily lives. Like Christians today, they quickly recognized that belief in Christ's redemptive message did not mean there would be no more problems, so they wanted help in learning how to live their lives after their conversion. Because Jesus never commented publicly about the subject of Christians being married to non-Christians, they looked to Paul for guidance.

Perhaps some of the Corinthian Christians had read the account of Ezra 10:10–15, which records Ezra's chastising of the Hebrew men who had taken pagan wives during the time when many Jews were deported to Babylon. Wanting to reestablish respect for Yahweh's laws, Ezra instructed that all the pagan wives and their children should be removed from Israelite families, and all but two men chose to comply with these instructions. Could it be that the new Corinthian Christians were fearful that God would require similar measures from them? We do not know the actual impetus for

their questions, but apparently the subject of mixed marriage created enough of a controversy that they felt the need for clarification.

When Paul responded to the Corinthians' question, his manner
was parallel to that of Christ. By the Holy Spirit's prompting, He was
encouraging believers to discover God's loftiest principles of living,
making that their ultimate goal. In a subsequent chapter of his letter to the Corinthians, he taught, "All things are lawful." He wanted
the Corinthians to realize that they were free to make whatever
choice they wanted regarding their life's priorities. He quickly followed that statement with another: "but not all things are profit-
able." That is, he wanted believers to make decisions that would
reflect a godly witness.

Let's take a closer look at the situation that prompted Paul's
comments about divorce in a marriage where one spouse is a Christian and the other is not.

Corinth was a city known for its loose living, perhaps in a similar
way to modern New Orleans or Amsterdam. Loose self-expression,
parties, sexual freedoms, and carousing were a natural part of the city's
vibrancy. Corinth was a prosperous place where many merchants
manufactured and traded wares on an international scale. There was
plenty of affluence, which allowed its citizens to pursue self-gratifying
behavior. Also, Corinth was the home to the temple of Aphrodite,
the Greek goddess of love. There at the temple were hundreds of prostitutes looking for men who would worship at the altar of sexual in-
dulgence, joining with them in drunkenness and debauchery. Of
course, not all Corinthian people were so extreme, but as anyone
today can attest, when a large segment of people in one place prioritize sexuality and carousing above all else, the philosophy can have a
major spillover effect on the surrounding people. Certainly Corinth
was a place where godlessness permeated the culture.

Into this atmosphere came Paul, teaching the supremacy of Christ
and His emphasis on humility, goodness, and kindness. I can only
imagine the reception of Paul's teachings as he spoke about such a radically different approach to life. Put God first? Consider your life as
dead? Let Christ be your guide? Consider others as more important
than yourself? Honor sexual purity? Yet these were the themes he

taught, and we can rest assured that this teaching was like no other instruction that had taken root in this city of licentiousness.

Think for a moment how one family might be affected if the wife becomes a Christian, fully embracing this radically different philosophy of life. At the same time, her husband openly scorns "The Way" as a cultic sect that he cannot tolerate. Suppose, then, that the wife attends meetings two or three times a week with this Christian group, making new friends and developing a very different set of priorities. The husband continues seeing his same old drinking buddies; his chief concern, as it had has been for years, is to find the next party. The children, of course, witness the vast difference developing between their parents' priorities. Imagine the awkwardness they experience as they wonder which lifestyle they should imitate. They surely feel the confusion of knowing that their choices will displease one of the parents. They have a no-win situation on their hands.

With this type of scenario being common within the young Corinthian church, the leaders apparently wrote Paul to receive an opinion from him. "What should we do when one spouse is a Christian and the other remains firmly entrenched in the old lifestyle? Is it better to divorce under these uncomfortable conditions?" That was the impetus for Paul's remarks.

Paul surely had witnessed this building problem during the months that he spent in Corinth, and he probably knew many of the individuals trapped in this dilemma. He certainly wanted the Christians there to have the least amount of trauma or disruption in their family lives. Likewise, he wanted them to make choices that would enhance their witness in the community. His response therefore was to instruct that they should maintain marriage if at all possible. Because God places such a high priority on marital harmony, Paul wanted the Christians to show that they would do whatever they could to uphold such God-ordained values. If the unbelieving spouse was not clamoring to leave the marriage, the Christian mate should continue to honor the marriage, even though the union lacked a joint commitment to God.

In stating that the Christian spouse was free if the unbeliever decided independently to leave, Paul was recognizing that they had not been united in the Lord anyway. This put their marriage on a different level than if they were both Christians. Paul knew that two believers could work more persistently to hold their marriage together because of the common bond in the Spirit, but the bond could not be found in a religiously mixed marriage.

Paul's teaching was consistent with Jesus' earlier thoughts about marriage and divorce. He recognized that God never likes to see anyone divorce and that God's highest ideal is for each husband and wife to approach the marital roles with reverence. This is why Paul urged Christians to stay within their marriage if at all possible. He wanted their lives to be a living illustration that a love for God's ways can make a positive difference in personal interactions.

The Stronger Person Makes the Greater Concessions

To get a deeper perspective of Paul's mind-set as he was communicating with the Corinthian church, it would be helpful to examine his further instructions in I Corinthians 8. This chapter addressed the dilemma of Christians eating meat butchered from animals previously sacrificed to idols. The more mature Christians recognized that meat is meat, and if the pagans chose to chant over it before preparing it for the marketplace, it was still meat fit for consumption. The less mature Christians felt it might offend God to eat this meat, so they chose to bypass it altogether. Paul's advice to the more mature Christians was to defer to the less mature Christians in order to save the integrity of the church fellowship (I Corinthians 8:1–13). He was less concerned about the hard musts or shoulds and more pragmatically focused on maintaining an atmosphere of love.

We can interpret his words in I Corinthians 7 about not divorcing in the same light. Paul was not so interested in issuing hard mandates as he was in being pragmatic while preserving the possibility of love. In Chapters 7 and 8 his emphasis was to place the responsibility squarely on the shoulders of the ones closest to the Lord to do whatever they could in order to set an example of sacrificial love. Rather than teaching law keeping for the sake of law keeping, he was teaching a mind-set of servitude and humility. In fact, this same teaching was most profoundly expressed later in that same letter, when he wrote, "If I have the gift of prophecy, and know all mysteries and all knowledge, and if I have all faith, so as to remove mountains, but do not have love, I am nothing" (I Corinthians 13:2). Rules, correctness, and superior knowledge were empty if people did not apply their beliefs with an attitude of godly love.

Let there be no doubt: the *ideal* is that no marriage should ever be dissolved. When two people choose to bind their lives together in holy matrimony, both should be wise and mature enough to know that marriage takes constant work, dedication, and sacrifice. Unfortunately, family life rarely unfolds in a neat and tidy manner. Unforeseen problems arise. People can and do fail, sometimes miserably. Selfishness and other psychological and spiritual problems can gain a foothold. The ideal unravels into a marital nightmare.

When God established the ideal of a nondissolvable marriage union, Adam and Eve knew no sin. Had they remained sinless they would have had no problem upholding the standard. When they sinned, however, two things became apparent. First, God's truth would forever remain true; He would not lower His standards. Second, God *immediately* displayed grace. He killed an animal and covered the two with its skin, signifying that an appropriate substitutionary death would remove the burden of having to be perfect in order to have fellowship with God. He never changed His principles of right and wrong, but He did make provision for fallen humans to remain in fellowship with Him.

Perfect Principles Are Nobler

As we ponder how Jesus and Paul referred to the question of divorce, let's recognize three key ideas that show the difference between their insistence upon being legally correct and the practice of professing perfection.

Condemnation Is Discouraged

I spoke with a man we'll call Brent, who had been a member of the ministerial staff in several prominent churches. When we talked, he was working at a secular job and was experiencing depression. It had been three years since Brent's divorce was finalized. He had no prospects or hope of ever returning to the ministry in his denomination. "I spent almost twenty-five years serving churches," he explained, "and without a doubt that's where my heart still lies. Many people came to know the Lord through my efforts, and many more came to know God more fully because of teaching and discipleship programs I managed. It was wonderful work and highly rewarding, but it all came to an end once I got divorced."

Brent went on to explain that his wife had originally shared his vision to serve God, but as the years passed she turned into a sour, worldly woman. Their communication dwindled down to almost nothing. For the last two years of their marriage, she lived on the opposite side of the house from Brent and would go weeks at a time without saying a word to him. When their youngest child left for college, she filed for divorce; he had not spoken with her since.

"It was hard trying to carry on in my work, knowing that my marriage was so painful, but now I'm freed from all that. Because I've been through this broken experience, I have a much deeper sense of compassion for hurting people. It's strange, but I've realized that my pain has made me a stronger person." Pausing for a moment, he added, "Most of the pastors in my denomination would express sympathy for what I've gone through, but they're afraid to take a chance on me. Either they are perplexed about how to handle the hiring of a divorced minister or they fear the repercussions from church members who would be upset about hiring someone like me. It's like I'm now branded for life as damaged goods."

Most Christian divorcees can relate all too well to the "damaged goods" label Brent describes. Virtually all of their Christian teaching emphasizes the need for godly values and a life that is consistent with scriptural teaching. Perhaps they are unaware of it at the time, but often these teachings are accompanied with implied musts, supposed tos, and have tos. It is these implications that form the foundation for a rejecting mind-set.

When the Pharisees were attempting to entice Jesus into a definitive pronouncement, part of the covert message was, "Tell us whom we can approve or reject." They knew that if Jesus met them on the legalistic playing field He would invariably renounce someone and create a reason for individuals to feel rejected by Him. That's what the narrower attitude accomplishes. It covertly communicates, "You have to be this way or else . . ."

Think back to your grammar school days, when every assignment received a grade. The standard was set, and then you attempted to meet it with good performance. Suppose, for instance, you took a mathematics test. You did the best you could, turned the work in, and then waited for your grade. Once you received the grade, a second round of measurement was set off. You were judged on the basis of the grade you received. If you made an A, your peers and your parents told you how terrific you were. If you made a D, you knew you would be judged as a dunce or a goof-off. Your internal peace could rise or fall, according to your ability to make the grade and keep your critics satisfied.

Likewise, divorcees have the double distinction of being graded poorly. First, they earn a flunking grade because the marriage failed. Then they have to face their inquisitors' grading them on the basis of the reason for the divorce. Instead of the biblical teaching being used as a guide for right living, it is used as a reason to condemn—which is simply not right. This runs contradictory to the Good News.

Beginning with Adam and Eve, God proved that He is not shocked when people fall short of His best. He does not give up His convictions; He chooses to continue loving despite those shortcomings. We too can love and fellowship with one another despite failures and poor judgments.

Perfect Principles Encourage Us

When I was a boy, my family had several children's books of stories that ultimately illustrated a truth that would enrich my life. I recall that my mother or dad read these stories to me and would then explain how I could live according to those principles if I concentrated on letting God guide me. Years later, when it was my turn to do the same with our two girls, I gave them the same message: "God has designed a wonderful way of life; you can find a great reward as you learn it and apply it."

Perfect principles give the growing child a goal to aim for. As a boy (and also now as a middle-aged man) I was imperfect in my implementation. Likewise, as our own girls are blossoming into womanhood, they too fall short. But each time anyone in our family misses the mark, we can upright ourselves knowing that despite the imperfection the ideal never changes. We may repeatedly fail, yet we can still return to God's standard. This is the joy of serving a God who has an understanding of the human heart.

When Jesus spoke to His followers, He did not teach in relative terms. That is, He did not say, "Do what you feel like doing for the moment and just rest upon that." He always held up the highest standard: "Know that I have a plan for you that is far and away better than any scheme produced by worldly minded people. Let Me teach it to you and encourage you to see that you can do better than what you have experienced so far." He was so serious about guiding His followers toward that standard that He commissioned the Holy Spirit to indwell and guide believers after His ascension to heaven.

As He presented His perfect principles, Jesus also showed an enormous capacity to love, even when people fell woefully short of the mark. This does not mean He never confronted or spurred them to choose better. He often goaded people to make a stronger effort. He did communicate often and powerfully, though, that He would continue to receive believers who knew His perfect principles yet were flawed in their efforts to live a consistent life.

A unique relationship between Jesus and a troubled divorcee illustrates His compassionate mind-set. John 4:5–42 records the story of Jesus' interaction with the woman at the well in Sychar who had been divorced five times. Sitting alone at the well outside town while the disciples were in town buying supplies, Jesus spoke cordially to the woman as she drew water. She immediately showed herself to be defensive and distrustful—likely results of a checkered history and being constantly judged for it. Jesus, though, was steady and calm as He spoke metaphorically about a type of water that would never run dry. He was alluding to cleansing salvation and the promise of the Holy Spirit. Not one to catch on to such abstract thinking, the woman remained skeptical and defensive.

In the middle of the conversation, Jesus asked her to go get her husband. When she replied that she had no husband, Jesus revealed His awareness of her five divorces (as well as her current live-in boyfriend). She responded with shock that He knew such things, but when Jesus returned to His message of redemption she was extremely receptive. Now He had her undivided attention.

Why did Jesus make it a point to introduce this embarrassing information about her history of broken relationships? This was His way of saying, "Ma'am, let's establish that I already know the rotten parts of your life, and it doesn't turn Me away. There's no need to be defensive around Me because I'll accept you as you are, five divorces and all." His message was one of hope. He did not want her flawed past to inhibit her from knowing the fullness of that hope.

Some people today might say, "Jesus showed acceptance for this woman's divorces, that's true; but she made her mistakes before becoming a believer, so that makes it different." The implication of this reasoning is that Jesus would not have shown the same grace to her if she had been a believer prior to being a divorcee. That, of course, is absurd; His grace is a blanket offer, given to both the saved and the unsaved. Yes, believers have knowledge that unbelievers do not, but they still carry imperfection and Christ is still willing to continue in grace before, during, and after the first moment of salvation.

God's perfect principles are meant to edify. They are given to show that a life yielded to Christ can produce better results than a life driven by sinful pride. If Christians receive those principles and commit themselves to God's will, good things can come to their lives. If those principles are violated, pain may result and difficulties may follow, yet Christ still remains available to love them and continue pointing them in the right direction.

When today's Christians scorn fellow believers who are divorced, they make the grave error of forgetting that they too are believers who fall short of God's standard for perfection every day. Their failing may not be in the marital arena, but it is in some other part of their life, guaranteed. It is risky, then, for one Christian to say to another, "You are not worthy of fellowship with me because I don't like the nature of your failure."

God does not give us perfect teachings only then to decrease the amount of grace we can receive according to our awareness of the truthfulness of those teachings. He gives us instructions and is fully aware that He will also continue loving us until He calls us to be at home with Him for all eternity. At that point, and only then, will we be able to sustain His perfect principles.

The Personal Dimension Is Emphasized

When Christians speak to people like Brent about how they *must* manage their difficult situations, they inevitably bypass the personal struggles and treat them solely as people who are supposed to perform in a specific way. I have heard comments from these wounded people that reflect the heartache of being on the receiving end of judgmental scrutiny:

> "They have no idea how much I've agonized about my marital problems. No one seems to care that I've prayed fervently over this."

> "There has been so much pain in my life that I can't overlook, yet those folks are so consumed with fitting me into the mold that they won't listen to my feelings."

> "I was married to someone who clearly quit! Why am I getting the blame for saying that I couldn't handle that?"

> "The people who are most critical toward me have problems of their own that create a poor witness, but because they haven't been divorced I guess they feel justified in condemning me. It must mean that divorcees are lower than other sinners."

> "People assume that because I'm divorced, the rest of my Christian life is a smokescreen. It's like I don't get credit for still taking God seriously."

As I read New Testament accounts of Jesus or Paul interacting with individuals, I sense their deep yearning to connect on a very personal level. Love is preeminent. They both loved the Law yet were willing to overlook flaws when there was an opportunity to connect with others lovingly. Jesus, for instance, touched a leper, though he would be ceremonially unclean. He spoke gently to a known adulterer. He dined with men who made a living cheating people at taxes. He was friendly to the five-time divorcee. Paul too emphasized the supremacy of love, as he implored his flock to drink from the fountain of the love of God that he had been privileged to know.

I recall one man who received a call from a friend who heard of his divorce. The friend invited him to dinner and in their conversation explained: "The reason for your divorce is a matter between you and God. I'm sorry you're experiencing the painful fallout, but I want you to know that I hold you in the highest regard. My desire right now is to know how I can pray for you. I want to help you keep your focus on the fact that you're God's special person." The divorced man openly wept as he told his friend, "You are the only person who has spoken to me like this, and I appreciate it greatly."

Every divorced person needs messages of love. In the aftermath of a marital split, they have experienced heartache, anger, loneliness, rejection, and embarrassment. The *last* thing this person needs is someone speaking sternly about which rules were or were not kept. As they experience God's love, they have myriad opportunities to learn about His perfect principles. The Holy Spirit can bring conviction regarding areas of shortcoming. In the meantime, the vehicle that can carry them to know God's ways most fully is the tenderness and kindness of those who would say, "I've been in the place of needing someone to accept me as I am, hurts and all; therefore, I gladly pass along to you the grace that God has given to me."

Chapter Six

Mercy's Priority

Several years ago I was approached by a man who made an unusual request. His adult daughter was in the county jail on charges related to white-collar criminal activities. She was five months pregnant and had just received word that her husband had caused the death of her two-year-old daughter. To say she was traumatized would be a gross understatement. This man was asking if I would be willing to counsel her at the jail facility.

The request posed two problems. First, I would have to be cleared by the judge overseeing the case before I could be granted permission to meet with her. Second, I never conducted house calls, much less visits to a jail. I would have to shift gears mentally and physically to accommodate her. Despite these oddities, we decided to petition the court to allow me to see this woman, and permission was indeed granted. Once that hurdle was cleared, I made special arrangements in my schedule and saw her six times at the jail before she was released. We continued our counseling at my office, and it turned out to be one of my most interesting and rewarding cases. Being at the very lowest point of her life, this woman made herculean efforts to change and grow.

About fifteen years after my work with her concluded, I received a phone call from the same woman, asking if I remembered her. Of course I did, and it was wonderful to hear from her again. She brought me up to date on her new marriage and family life, and then she told me the real reason for her call: "For years I have had very warm thoughts regarding the counseling I did with you. As I look back on the way you made adjustments so you could help me, I'm still amazed that you were willing to do what you did. I just wanted to thank you again for being kind enough to do something out of the ordinary when I needed it most."

As I go about my work of helping people, I have a protocol that I use with my clients. If I do not adhere to consistent policies and procedures, my life easily becomes chaotic since my work does not lend itself to an off-the-cuff approach. Every now and then, however, an unusual circumstance presents itself that does not fit my protocol, yet it nonetheless warrants my attention. When confronted with such circumstances, my sense of good will can prompt me to consider another path because I have an obligation, to myself and my clients, to maintain wise business practices, but an even higher desire to be an embodiment of goodness and grace. Sometimes the higher desire overrides strict adherence to protocol.

Jesus' Emphasis on Weightier Matters

Without question, a goal of Jesus' ministry was the presentation of God's perfect principles for successful living. Jesus believed in order and greatly respected the laws and customs that were a framework for such success. It comes as no surprise, though, to see that there were times when He would set aside the exactness required by the Law in order to address a greater issue. Let's look briefly at a few examples of how He handled awkward circumstances that might have caused Him to choose adherence to the Law at the expense of mercy toward the individual. Then we can learn from His approach how His mind-set might influence our examination of the way we can respond to people who have divorced under awkward circumstances.

David's Use of Consecrated Bread

Matthew 12:1–8 records a scene where the Pharisees chided Jesus and His disciples for harvesting grain and eating it on the Sabbath. They were convinced that this was work, which was not to be done on the Sabbath. In response, Jesus cited a story that is recorded in I Samuel 21:1–6. David, on the run from his tormentor, Saul, encountered the priest Ahimelech. His men were hungry and in need of provisions, so David pressed the priest for assistance. The only bread the priest had to offer was bread that had been consecrated to the Lord according to the Levitical Law (described in Leviticus 24:5–9). This bread could be eaten only by priests, and only one week following the consecration. Given the fact, though, that these men were in genuine need and that this bread was the only food available, David and Ahimelech made the logical decision and allowed the men to eat the bread.

As Jesus referred to this incident, He condoned David's decision (and His own decision to "harvest" on the Sabbath) by explaining that something greater than the temple Law was at stake. Quoting from the prophet Hosea, He reminded His detractors that God desires "compassion, not sacrifice." Though the Law appropriately addressed matters of worship, clean living, and liturgy, Jesus was emphasizing that human needs takes precedence. Service to God is not in adherence to rules for the sake of adhering to rules; it involves ministry to real humans at their point of need.

To emphasize His point, on the same day Jesus went to a synagogue where there was a man with a withered hand (Matthew 12:9–14). Challenging the Pharisees, He asked if it would be lawful to heal him on the Sabbath. Knowing that He would provoke their wrath, Jesus healed him on the spot; then He referred to the Law's allowance for a sheep to be removed from a pit on the Sabbath, saying, "Of how much more value then is a man than a sheep!" His love compelled Him to give priority to kindness even if it meant that He would sidestep strict interpretation of the Sabbath rules. Clearly, Jesus was bold in asserting that the Law is necessary, up to a point. When it interferes with giving mercy and assistance, the Law may be momentarily superseded by the gift of goodness.

The Ox That Needs Water

In a similar scene, recorded in Luke 13:10–17, Jesus encountered a woman in a synagogue with a severely bent back. Knowing that this condition had existed eighteen years, and having compassion for her,

Jesus placed His hands on her and she was able once again to stand erect. As she expressed praises to God, the religious official scolded Jesus for healing on the Sabbath. "There are six days in which work should be done; therefore come during them and get healed, and not on the Sabbath day."

Jesus' response was pointed. He reminded him that the Law allowed people to untie an ox or a donkey to lead it toward water on the Sabbath. Surely it would also allow Him to release this woman from her infirmity. Though the religious leaders in this story were described as humiliated by Jesus' words and actions, it is recorded that the rest of the observers were quite merry because of what He had done. Once again, Jesus was appealing to a higher principle. Without dismissing the Law's validity, He illustrated that there are times when discretion allowed Him the liberty to place greater value on alleviation of human suffering. Never did He state that the Law was unimportant. His actions, however, indicated that He was willing to be flexible in order to allow the message of mercy to be fully communicated.

Tithing the Spice Cabinet

Matthew 23 records what could be described as the most stinging words Jesus ever spoke to the keepers of the Law. In verse 23, He speaks strongly to the religious leaders about the upside down way they maintained priorities. "You tithe mint and dill and cumin," He said, "and have neglected the weightier provisions of the Law: justice and mercy and faithfulness."

Can you imagine the meticulous precision that had to be maintained to accurately measure exactly one tenth of each of the spices used for cooking? Such a notion of tithing could be understood as legitimate since Leviticus 27:30 actually called for tithing of produce grown on the land. "Thus all the tithe of the land, of the seed of the land of the fruit of the tree, is the Lord's. It is holy to the Lord." The religious rulers of Jesus' day, however, took this principle to mean that even if you owned a very small portion of a crop it too was subjected to the Law. So insistent were they that the Law must be kept that no detail could escape their scrutiny. In the effort to be precise, they eventually lost their sensitivity to human realities.

In exposing this practice, Jesus was emphasizing that God had never intended for the Law to be so dominant that it required them to set aside logic or common sense. It was logical to tithe the proceeds from a crop of mint or dill or cumin, but when they insisted that they must tithe once it made its way into the spice cabinet, they were turning the Law into an unnecessary burden. Jesus did not want us to be so focused on correctness for the sake of correctness that we lost the capacity to recognize that God wants us to have goodness in our hearts.

It's About Priorities

In none of His comments did Jesus disparage the Law. He held it in highest regard, and He lived by its provisions in His personal life. Yet when forced to choose between strict adherence to the Law and the ministry of grace to a person in need, Jesus' pattern is clearly discernible. He gave priority to personal needs.

Imagine the plight of the leper, for instance, whose encounter with Jesus is recorded in Matthew 8:1–4. In those days, a leper was required by the Law (see Leviticus 13:45–59) to remove himself from his family and community. He was to live in isolation, touching no one and allowing no one to touch him. His leprosy rendered him ceremonially unclean. The leper in this story was quite bold as he drew near enough to Jesus to ask Him for healing. Remarkably, Matthew's account says that Jesus stretched out His hand and touched him.

Faithful Jews who observed Jesus touching a leper might have gasped and shouted, "Jesus, you can't do that! You're not supposed to touch a leper until he is thoroughly scrutinized by the priest!" Setting aside the Law's requirement, Jesus was making a bold statement through His use of touch. In essence, He communicated: "With all due respect to the Law, I have a greater message that I want this man to know. Despite his unclean state, I love him through and through. There is no more profound way to demonstrate My love than to touch him and bring healing not only to his body, but to his spirit."

Jesus loved the Law. But He loved people even more!

When we as Christians read scriptural instructions about the sanctity of marriage and about the undesirable nature of divorce, it is always wisest to respect it and to yield to God's direction regarding the subject. It is never pleasing to God when we seemingly shrug our shoulders regarding His principles, casually dismissing the seriousness of the subject. Following the example of Jesus, though, if we encounter people who have fallen short of perfection we need not hold so tightly to the principle that the weightier human matter is ignored. We do not belittle God's teaching when we choose to love someone who does not conform perfectly to God's plan. Instead, we show them Christ's grace!

Repeatedly, the church is faced with the question of how to respond to individuals who are divorcing for reasons other than adultery or a nonbeliever's abandonment. Too often it is tempting to focus on the reason for the divorce, ignoring the spiritual and emotional needs that could be addressed. If we choose, however, to concentrate primarily on the personal dimensions, we open the door for the possibility of ministering on a much broader scale.

Sydney was a woman in her late thirties who was in the midst of a taxing divorce. Her soon-to-be-ex-husband seemed to turn every discussion into a verbal sparring match, a pattern that had existed throughout most of their marriage. No conversation with him was easy, yet she had to keep the lines of communication open because they had kids' schedules to coordinate and business matters to address. In our first two counseling sessions, we discussed her personal history and the various trouble spots she was encountering; we laid out some broad outlines regarding how she could begin to learn to manage her mixed bag of emotions.

During my third visit with Sydney, she made a telling comment. "I've told you why Ben and I are divorcing," she said, "but you haven't really made an issue of the fact that there were no sexual sins involved. My last counselor kept pushing to get me to take Ben back because she felt I should somehow be able to hold the marriage together. Help me understand the approach you're using with me."

Sydney did not realize it, but she had just opened the door for me to share a message of grace. "I want you to know that I have a bias toward seeing marriages succeed, as opposed to witnessing a divorce," I explained. "Before I can talk with you intelligently, though, about what is happening in your life, I need to know and understand *you*. When you first spoke with me about your dilemma, I could tell that you were greatly hurt; I want to see if we can first get a feeling for what is behind that hurt. When you feel more whole as an individual, you'll be more suited to make a wise decision about how to proceed with your marriage."

She remained silent for a moment and then commented, "In my community, everyone has been so busy trying to determine who is more at fault for our marital problems that no one has made a genuine effort to hear my heart." She began weeping as she then said, "Thank you for taking the time to know me."

There is a time in any marital crisis to be concerned with policies and procedures or the game plan. Yet even as we feel the need to scrutinize those logistics in a divorce case, we do best when we remember that the individuals involved are probably experiencing some of the most traumatizing emotions they will ever have to face. These are people whose lives are being turned upside down. They are prime candidates for a caring arm around the shoulder. More than ever, they need kind words from caring people who are more interested in the person than the procedure. This does not negate the need to seriously explore issues of right and wrong. It merely underscores that emotional and spiritual healing comes when the human dimension is given priority.

For us to approximate Jesus' emphasis on the person over the rules, let's examine four key ideas that are crucial to the ministry of grace.

Limit Human Suffering

Human suffering need not go on longer than necessary. Recall Jesus' comments about pulling a sheep out of a hole or about guiding an ox or a donkey to water on the Sabbath. Though respecting the principle of Sabbath rest, Jesus taught that animals had needs that could supersede an owner's desire to rest and the rules concerning proper observation of the Sabbath. Rather than showing disdain toward God's teaching when tending to the animal's needs, they would be demonstrating goodness and kindness to the animal.

Most people in the throes of divorce do not make a decision to separate for frivolous reasons. Sometimes immaturity is involved in the decision; many times it is not. The tension leading to the separation may have included abusive anger, addictive behavior, gross neglect, or chronic condescension. To focus only on the correctness of the divorce procedures is to miss an opportunity to extend love to the one in great pain.

When Sydney expressed gratitude that I had made the effort to understand her needs and perspectives, I felt a mixed reaction. First, I was pleased that I was in a position to demonstrate grace. I try never to take for granted that I get to be an instrument to show the Lord's good will when I encounter someone like her who is struggling to make sense of a collapsed dream. Second, however, I felt frustrated because I realized that too many divorcees encounter Christians in fear that they will be shunned because they have missed the mark. Many people, like Sydney, learn that their pain will be overlooked, as if it is nonexistent.

Marriage as presented in scripture shows that a husband's and wife's love for each other can become an experiential picture of God's undying devotion to His beloved. Most Christian men and women begin marriage with great optimism that they are entering a relationship that will enhance godly joy and minimize loneliness. Divorcees find, however, that the promise of finding godly love in marriage becomes less and less likely as isolation, contention, and invalidation grow. Those disappointments hurt!

By the time the couple reaches the point of divorce, the hurt is unbearable. Outside observers may feel uncomfortable with the decision to pursue divorce, but the divorcing person is nevertheless in agony because hope has given way to futility. It is the feeling of futility that needs to be addressed. This is what Jesus was willing to do when He straightened the woman's back, healed the man's withered arm, and touched the pleading leper. His message was clear: "I see inside your emotions. I am sorry that you have struggled with your pain. My love for you is so strong that I'll give highest priority to ministering to you at your point of need."

Missing the mark of God's perfect standard is not a desirable thing. Living a life of pain and torment is also not desirable. Before we can make inroads in motivating people to learn to incorporate God's provision for successful living, we do best to let them know we do not want them to feel unnecessarily disparaged. Only when this merciful message is registered can the individual trust that the rest of the message is worthy of consideration.

Use Common Sense

Common sense has a place in discerning how to proceed. Imagine how coldhearted the church official sounded when Jesus healed the woman with the bent back, with the official instructing that on any other day the healing might be satisfactory but not on the Sabbath. Common sense would suggest that the day set aside to contemplate the Lord is a reasonable time to offer a message regarding God's kindness, particularly if the opportunity is on full display. Jesus would have seemed quite petty had He said, "Sorry ma'am, but you'll have to see if you can catch up with Me tomorrow. I'm not allowed to show goodness on the Sabbath. . . . I'm busy worshipping God today."

A high percentage of divorces occur because the negative ingredients are so prevalent that one or both partners have lost hope. For instance, I learned that Sydney's marriage was typified for years by heated arguments and a seemingly chronic adversarial atmosphere. "Ben seemed to have lost any willingness to treat me with dignity," she explained. "It was not at all uncommon for him to treat me poorly in front of the children, to the point where cursing and name calling became a familiar scene. The kids learned to live in fear of him. We each dreaded the times when Ben and I had to do things together because no one trusted that anything good would come from our efforts. I'll have to be honest and admit that I finally learned to dish out to him some of the critical sentiments he gave to me. I'm not proud to say it, but eventually I could be just as negative as he was."

Sydney became convinced that she needed to change her attitude and behavior, so several months prior to her divorce she sought counseling. She told me: "Going to counseling was the best thing that could happen to me because I was challenged to look honestly at myself like never before. I learned that I did not need to allow Ben or anyone else to set the tempo for my life. I could be a healthy person as I chose to let God guide my life. Repeatedly I asked Ben to go to counseling with me, but he refused. In fact, as time progressed his anger became more intense as our home life worsened. I was finding hope and healing, but at the same time we were growing farther and farther apart."

Sydney's divorce was not prompted by adultery or abandonment by a nonbeliever, so it failed to meet the "technical" requirements of New Testament teaching. Yet when an abusive or hateful atmosphere abounds, common sense indicates that it is reasonable to seek relief from chronic dysfunction, particularly if efforts to find relief fail repeatedly. We would like to see marital healing rather than divorce, but we do not show disloyalty to God's teachings by lovingly supporting those who are in such a predicament.

Find Unique Responses

Unique problems may point to unique responses. When a father asked me to visit his daughter in the county jail, I could have reasoned that anyone playing loose with the law needs to be prepared for whatever fallout comes their way. It would not have been outrageous for me to have told this father that I was unable to accommodate his request because of its unusual nature.

I could have maintained a clear conscience in turning down this request, but a compelling thought caused me to bend my own rules of protocol. I could tell from the father's demeanor that he and his daughter were at a crossroads. Having lost her two-year-old child, pregnant, in jail, facing the uncertainty surrounding her legal problems, this woman was potentially at a defining moment in her life. Indeed, subsequent events proved that she was ready as never before to encounter God and make Him real in her life. If I had played it by the book, I would have missed a wonderful opportunity to be a conduit for God's mercy. Who knows what this woman might have felt or done? Sometimes thinking outside the box can create possibilities for powerful healing.

In healing the sick on the Sabbath and excusing David's men for eating consecrated bread, Jesus was not displaying a casual attitude regarding God's procedures. Rather, He was looking beyond the momentary matter into the unique circumstances that called for an unusual response. Knowing that these individuals did not ask for their maladies, He chose to consider how their lives could be improved even if it meant that He made an exception to the Law. Rather than making decisions based upon predetermined criteria uniformly applied, He chose to make His decisions case by case. He was wise enough to know that extenuating circumstances must be considered when determining how to respond to needs.

Christians can inadvertently back themselves into a corner of malice by categorically condemning people who divorce for reasons that seem not to make sense. For instance, to an outside observer, a woman who divorces her husband because he has refused for years to work and plays video games at home every day may not have just grounds for divorce. Encountering such a case, I am willing to defer judgment as I consider extenuating circumstances. The Bible is silent on the subject of divorce for chronic laziness, irresponsibility, or disinterest. It could certainly be appropriate for a spouse to want relief from such a distasteful predicament, and it would certainly be wise to pray and seek godly counsel regarding the best path to take. Besides, it is not my prerogative to play the role of the Holy Spirit. I could certainly speak with such a person about her options, but ultimately I need to allow her to respond to her understanding of the Holy Spirit's prompting.

Jeremiah 34:8–22 describes a strong reaction from God regarding Israelites who reneged on a covenant to release slaves they possessed. King Zedekiah entered into a solemn agreement with the citizens that they would release slaves, and that it would no longer be legal to hold a fellow countryman in bondage. All of the people initially agreed to and obeyed the stipulation of the covenant, but over time some of the citizens chose to revert to their slave-holding practices. In the end, the ones who reneged on the covenant were given over to enemies of the state and experienced sad consequences for their choice.

Don't many marriages fail because at least one partner chooses not to live according to the covenant vows made at the time of the marital union? Like the people of Jeremiah's day, they may originally pledge loyalty to God's model and then over time change course. In essence, a spouse who lives outside the norms of the covenant of love, honor, and obedience has chosen to disavow the original marital contract. Could it be that it is appropriate for the offended spouse to separate from the one who has chosen to break the contract? Divorcing does not fit the desires of the Lord, but maintaining fellowship with one who has chosen to renege on a holy covenant is not desirable to God either. It might require us to allow leeway under such circumstances.

As in biblical times, our world often produces circumstances that do not fit neatly into a predictable category. When a relationship is in serious trouble, people need friends who are willing to be a healing presence, not a judge who forces rules upon them.

Risk the Extraordinary

Sometimes there's a risk in weighing out-of-the-ordinary circumstances.

In each case where Jesus contradicted the Law in order to meet an unusual human need, He risked offending someone or sending a message that might be misconstrued. Certainly the Pharisees were offended by His willingness to think outside the box, but it was also possible that some common folks were perplexed too. Jesus was clearly a holy man who embodied God's character fully; but He almost seemed to look for opportunities to make a statement that showed He would not be bound by the Law. Though Jesus was indeed a scandalous figure of sorts, it is not likely that He wanted to fuel an atmosphere of cynicism for all established tradition. Even as He showed that He could be a free thinker, He also taught respect for the established order.

If we declare that there may be some unusual or extenuating circumstances that warrant compassion toward divorcees, there is a risk of some construing such thought as license. I recall one man who left his wife because he was "ready for a new adventure." The wife had good morals and she was committed to personal growth and marital harmony, but the husband left her because he had become bored and desired new stimulation. With a wide grin and a gleam in his eye, he excitedly said, "Isn't God's grace wonderful!" He was making a very poor decision, leaving a wife who was devoted to working with him in finding a satisfactory middle ground, and he was claiming that grace was a blessing that allowed him to feel good about his decision.

God's grace *is* wonderful, but it does not negate the seriousness of His laws. Maturity and discernment are most necessary when trying to determine how to proceed amid distasteful marital circumstances. Wherever divorce is mentioned in the scriptures, it is discussed in the context of its deviation from God's perfect standard. His grace allows for times when the standard is missed; still, it is this same grace that causes Him to refer us to the perfect standard of marital union. His love compels Him to compel us to seek lofty goals, and any determination to use that grace lightly brings grief to the One who desires the best for His own.

Be deeply grateful for His gifts of mercy and grace, while simultaneously seeking to follow His standards as closely as possible.

Chapter Seven

Grace Is Radical

Gwen, a single mom in her late thirties, was attempting to talk with me about the depression that had brought her to my office, but she was having a hard time getting the words out. With her hair pulled neatly into a tight bun, she wore a perfectly tailored royal blue suit that had become her standard for a new life in the commercial real estate business. She loved her work because it afforded her a good living while also giving her the flexibility to take out the time needed to keep up with the activities of her eighth grade daughter. The two had moved into a garden home three years earlier, and they seemed to be doing well in the aftermath of Gwen's split with her former husband.

Trying to find the words to express her frustration with herself, Gwen told me, "I was very angry with my husband because he had gotten involved with another woman at the end of our marriage. I was disgusted that he could be so loose with his sense of morality. At the time, I felt a real sense of superiority over him. I would never have stooped as low as he did. I would never have been unfaithful. What's more, I wasn't very silent. I told plenty of people what a sorry excuse for a human he was. I strongly disliked him for what he did to me."

Tears filled Gwen's eyes as she continued. "About three months ago, I had sexual relations with a man, and I've been filled with regret ever since." She paused to look carefully at me to gauge my reaction. Seeing compassion on my face, she ventured on. "It's bad enough that I was promiscuous because that makes me a hypocrite after all the mean things I said about my former husband, but there's more to the story." The tears flowed freely now as she had to grab a couple of tissues to gain her composure.

"I'm going to tell you something that is very shameful, and I wish I didn't have to say this." She paused, took a couple of deep breaths and explained, "The reason I had sex with him was because he was a customer I was working with. I was trying to close a deal. We had gone to dinner, had some wine, and the conversation got very friendly, and before you know it, he was flirting with me. The thought entered my mind that if we had sexual relations I knew I'd get him to agree to our business deal and there would be a very nice commission check waiting for me." She began crying uncontrollably.

I was quiet for a moment as I just let her have an uninterrupted moment to weep. I spoke gently, "This is obviously hard for you to talk about, but I'd like to hear more."

Gathering her composure, Gwen said, "Well, it happened just as I thought it would. Two nights in a row we slept together, and soon we had him signing a contract and writing out a fat check. When my boss congratulated me later and asked how I had been able to pull off such a lucrative deal single-handedly, I wanted to throw up." The tears flowed again. As before, I remained patient and spoke words of comfort.

By now, her face was quite red and she looked haggard, a far cry from the perfectly manicured persona she presented to the professional world. "There's more I have to tell you." So I remained quiet, letting her gather the strength to say what she needed to say. "In just a few weeks I learned I was pregnant. It was my worst nightmare, because I felt so humiliated and stupid. This man lived out of state, and I wouldn't be seeing him for months, and for that matter, I didn't *want* to see him. As far as I was concerned, I had become a whore. I had knowingly prostituted myself to get a big check. Do you know, he is the only person besides my husband I'd ever had sex with? I acted like a tramp and now I got what I had coming. I was pregnant."

I spoke calmly, saying: "Gwen, I imagine you have started a path toward soul searching like you've never been on before. I can only imagine what kind of tailspin that must have thrown you into as you contemplated how you would tell your daughter, family, and friends. Wow, what a predicament!"

Her voice grew stronger as she said, "Well, that leads to the rest of my story. I *didn't* tell my daughter, family, or friends. I didn't tell the man I had slept with either. As soon as I could I had an abortion. I just went on my own and did it." She broke down in tears again. Wailing out she cried, "I'm the lowest of all low people!"

I gave Gwen time to gather herself, and we spent the rest of the time discussing how she had sunk into a depression. She told me of her symptoms and how her life had become so different from the one she led in years past. "You have to understand, this is extremely different from the way it's been in the past. I have been very active in my church, teaching kids and being involved in Bible studies. My life was full of good friends, and I felt I was on track in living for God. But now I feel so distant from Him, like I've disqualified myself from ever receiving His goodness again. I am one huge phony! I can't tell you how miserable it is for me to be me."

The next week, Gwen came back to my office and opened with a confession that really made me think: "Before we get started, I want to tell you something. A friend of mine was aware that I was depressed, and she is the one who gave me your name for counseling. When she told me you were a Christian, I immediately had major reservations about coming to see you because I was afraid you'd be pretty hard on me. My friend kept insisting that I should come anyway, so I decided to take the chance and tell you my story."

"Tell me more about the nature of your reservations."

"Well, it's bad enough that I strayed sexually," Gwen said, "but it was extremely awkward to admit that I prostituted myself. Then to tell you I got pregnant and had an abortion . . ." Her voice trailed off and she just shook her head. "There's no way I would ever tell anyone at my church or in my family those things; they're so awful. I braced myself for a pretty stiff lecture from you, and believe me, I deserve it. There's no way I can ever live down my shame, especially about the fact that I took away the life of an innocent baby." The tears flowed again.

"Let's understand something right up front," I said to Gwen. "I'm here to help you heal. Right now it's evident that you need a very large dose of acceptance, so that's what I'm offering you. There's plenty of work ahead of us in the weeks to come, but in the meantime remember that the minute you walk in this door you will have the highest worth placed upon you. God loves you dearly, and it is my privilege to be a conduit for that love."

"I'm amazed," came her reply, "because that's foreign to anything I ever experienced with any of my past Christian friends. I can guarantee that there'd be a long line of people ready to stone me if I told most people everything I told you."

On the one hand, I was pleased that Gwen felt brave enough to take the chance to tell me what she had done. None of us is immune to the possibility of making really bad decisions. I looked forward to helping her use this experience in her life as a springboard for major growth. On the other hand, I was disturbed that she would fear my Christian beliefs making me unsafe. In fact, Gwen is not an isolated case. Numerous people have made similar statements to me through the years, expressing guardedness about the potential of being scorned because their behavior had strayed outside Christian norms. Of all the people in the world, a Christian should be the *first* that Gwen would tell her problems to.

Let's establish some convictions here. Am I in favor of sexual relations outside the commitment of marriage? No. Am I in favor of a businessperson using sex as a manipulative ploy to close a deal? Of course not. Do I believe abortion is a good way to sidestep an unwanted pregnancy? Definitely not. Do I believe that God's grace is deep enough and wide enough to cover Gwen's sins? Absolutely!

It is right and necessary that Christians know the principles given by God in order for goodness to prevail. Not one of God's commands brings harm to the person seeking to find a life of peace. God is a God of discernment, and His pronouncements are anchored in logic. Just as it is necessary to seek the Lord's guidance for lifestyle choices, it is equally necessary to recognize that God is not shocked when humans make poor choices. Because every person is certain to fail, and because God is also certain to prioritize love over rules, we can be sure that grace is available every time a person fails. When a struggler seeks Him out in a spirit of contrition and repentance, God stands ready to offer grace even before we realize the need for it. The giving of perfect laws illustrates God's deep desire to teach His people a workable system of justice; life operates best within these parameters. The giving of grace in moments when people fall short of the standards of justice illustrates how enormously important it is to God that He be chiefly known as a giver of love.

Why Is Grace So Confounding?

Something is dreadfully wrong within Christianity when sinners (inside or outside the church) conclude that they cannot confess their problems to believers for fear of rejection and banishment. This is the opposite of the manner of Christ.

When I talk with people like Gwen who can hardly bear to think of confessing the depths of their sins to Christians, knowing it would bring sure scorn, I wonder: What is it about grace that makes it so difficult for many to embrace? Why do we Christians insist on justice so strongly that we lose sight of the overriding priority God places on grace?

Grace Equalizes the Playing Field

During my childhood my father spent most of his time in and out of prisons, drug rehab facilities, and mental institutions. Before you express pity for me, recognize that he was a chaplain and counselor, and at times he was a consultant to professionals in these facilities. Because of his work, he encountered some interesting characters who had a lifelong history of repetitive wrongdoing and just plain meanness. Beginning in the 1950s, he witnessed hangings, counseled the family members of some of society's most troubled people, and yes, saw some very unlikely prospects accept Christ as Savior.

I recall a time as a college student when I was home on break and decided to pay Dad a visit at his prison office. We had lunch in the mess hall, and I spoke freely with several inmates that I had met on previous visits. As I looked around, I noticed that Buck over there wore a paisley shirt that looked remarkably like one I used to wear. Then I saw that Jose sported some green plaid slacks just like my favorite polyester, bell-bottom slacks of a few years prior. Then I noticed that Mike had a tan jacket and, what do you know, the jacket had my initials on it!

Grinning, I looked at Dad and asked, "Hey, have you been emptying my closet again?" We laughed because it felt good to know that my favorite clothes were now someone else's prized possessions. During that time in my life, Dad and I enjoyed talking philosophically (we still do), so later he mentioned that I was fortunate that it was just my clothes that were in prison. Now understand, I had been a decent kid who only got sent to the principal's office once, so I asked him what he meant by that. He told me I was blessed to have a Christian home, solid friends, balanced instruction from a loving church, and God-given common sense. Had I felt the same influences on me as Buck, Jose, or Mike did, I might have responded in the same way they did to their less fortunate circumstances.

I have thought often about that conversation and come to realize just how right he was. No human can claim superiority over another. This same idea is part of the lesson Jesus had in mind when He gave the Sermon on the Mount. When He identified how each person is capable of lust or anger, He was emphasizing how we all differ on the outside but are similar on the inside. Every one of us is in desperate need of grace.

One man spoke with me about his feelings regarding a Christian couple he knew who had just divorced. Though he barely knew me, he was free in dispensing his thoughts. "I'll tell you what, I used to like those people because I thought they were decent and upstanding, but my opinion of them, especially the husband, has gone way down."

I asked him why he felt so strongly and he spouted: "No Christian with any character would do something like getting a divorce. They've just become pawns of the devil."

After he rambled on with more negative comments, I interrupted him: "I have befriended each of them. Now more than ever, they need loving companionship."

To this he scoffed, "What they need is a swift kick in the butt."

What was going on here? This man clearly assumed that he was in a morally advantaged position over divorcees. Not willing to acknowledge his own vulnerability to pain or failure, he was incapable of being a conduit for grace.

To approach hurting fellow believers with love, it is first necessary to identify with that person's plight. Though I had never been convicted of a crime and sent to prison, I could relate with the prisoners as a college student because I knew that given the right set of circumstances I was capable of the same failings. In the same way, Christians who have never been divorced can nonetheless extend grace as they realize their own capacity for strife. Only when we see ourselves as equals who are differentiated by specific circumstances can we begin to look forward to giving one another grace. Judgmental people do not seem to be sensitive to the sad truth that at the core of our lives every one of us is a wretch who desperately needs the same daily outpouring of God's mercy.

Grace Requires an Admission of Vulnerability

One of the most familiar examples of Christ's display of grace is the story recorded in John 8:1–11, about a woman caught in the act of adultery. Surely you know it well. The Pharisees, who once again wanted to make Jesus appear foolish, brought this unnamed person before Christ in crude fashion. They asked Him to render a judgment about stoning her. His well-known response was to invite anyone without sin to cast the first stone; upon the withdrawal of the baffled Pharisees, He offered the wonderful gift of grace to the relieved woman. He did not condemn her.

The common response to Jesus' attitude is: "Wasn't that a nice thing for Jesus to say to that pathetic person?" We rightly assume that she must have had a deep history of problems and failures, because we can speculate that the Pharisees made sure they found a real loser to make their point with Jesus. We nod as we think, "It sure is reassuring to know that God can love someone as pitiable as this woman." Then perhaps we think, "I sure hope that lady cleaned up her act when she went home that day; she sure needed to do so."

It is entirely possible to miss the main thrust of the story of Jesus' encounter with this adulterous woman: *She represents me.* Whereas my sins may not be as openly displayed as hers, my need is just as great. Revelation 3:14–22 records God's words to the Laodicean church, an affluent church that seemed to be doing quite well. Rather than offering commendation to them, He says, "Because you say, 'I am rich, and have become wealthy, and have need of nothing,' you do not know that you are wretched and miserable and poor and blind and naked" (verse 17).

Not one Christian can justifiably stand in the presence of another human and state: "You oaf, you ought to wish you could be more together like me." Though our sins differ, our worth before God is the same in that it hinges entirely upon God's willingness to confer worth, and nothing else. No one has an ounce of moral worthiness outside the pronouncement of God.

One man, whom we'll call Daniel, spent his entire adult life serving in the church. He had a good reputation, a servant's heart, and a moral lifestyle. Most people had no clue that his marriage had been deteriorating for years. Unusual stress from experiences with extended family members caused Daniel and his wife to come under persistent tension. Their communication was not good. Distance seemed to be the only ingredient that kept them from unloading their pain on each other. After twenty-five years of marriage, they divorced. The wife moved to another state while Daniel remained in the church and community where he had lived during most of his adult life.

Daniel told me, "I was completely unprepared for the treatment I received after the news of my divorce went public. Some of my closest friends were kind and understanding, and they offered support in any way they could. But others suddenly treated me as if I were a hated criminal. I was told by one woman in the church that my life up to this point had been a fraud, that I was just another example of the hypocrisy that permeates today's church. Just last week I saw a man at the grocery store. We had served on committees together and prayed together for his troubled daughter years ago. I smiled and stopped to greet him, but he walked right past me as if I didn't exist. I was amazed! Another man called me on the phone and insisted that he would facilitate a meeting between myself and my ex-wife for the purpose of putting the marriage back together. I diplomatically explained that it was too late, but that we both welcomed his encouragement and prayer for the adjustments before us. He curtly said that it's never too late unless we were just quitters. Then he hung up on me."

As Daniel and I discussed these experiences, he told me: "The people who accept me as I am seem to realize that while they may or may not have had similar experiences, they too are unworthy aside from the gift of God's grace. The people who have been most rejecting seem to be operating on the assumption that they have value because they've kept the rules, and that I no longer have value because I broke the rules."

Today great emphasis is placed on being a winner, finding self-esteem, and living with confidence and happiness. This emphasis is not entirely wrong, since it is surely better to live in confidence than self-degradation. However, as people are claiming the blessings that God has offered them, it can be easy to forget that we deserve none of it. Each of us, on our own merit, has no reason to claim worthiness. The prophet Isaiah spoke the unflattering truth when he stated that each person is unclean, that our own righteousness is equivalent to filthy rags (Isaiah 64:6). Jeremiah was equally uncomplimentary when he said that the heart of each person is deceitful and desperately sick (Jeremiah 17:9). Yes, it is good to claim the high value that God has granted to each of us, but the ability to live humbly in such lofty status is enhanced by the realization that we are each pitiable without God's intervention. Our worth is a gift.

Christians who would scorn individuals such as Daniel or Gwen might easily say something like, "I realize my worth is a gift from God, but I cannot remain neutral when I see that someone is clearly letting their human shortcomings get out of control." When you hear the word *but* it usually indicates that the second portion of the sentence is given higher priority than the first. In this case, we could conclude that many would rather put an emphasis on correct performance and overlook the larger fact that no human has reason to boast of any goodness apart from God's grace.

Why was I able to be kind and accepting toward Gwen? My reasoning told me that although I had not committed exactly the sins she had, I have plenty of sinfulness in my own life that is unflattering. I've had troubles too. Strangely, my ability to love flows in direct proportion to my own willingness to admit my lack of perfect worthiness.

Christians who chide other Christians for falling short of God's perfect principles often have a poor memory. Their rejection of a fellow sinner illustrates that they have forgotten where they were when God found them. I applaud any Christian's fervor to uphold the standards of God's goodness *as long as* they can maintain a spirit of love. What good are high moral standards if accompanied by haughtiness and contempt? How can wounded believers recover and grow in an atmosphere of hostility and rejection?

I recall a man named Brian who was in great agony because he was struggling with the fallout of his marital split while his sister, Lissie, was being quite critical of the divorce. From the beginning of the marriage, Brian and his wife, Janie, seemed to be going in different directions. She was driven by her career, spending extra hours each day at work, whereas Brian wanted to have more personal time with her than she was willing to give. Over and over, the two argued about priorities and time commitments, but their exchanges would become predictably sour and the distance between them greater. After four years of feeling neglected, Brian finally told Janie they would have to adjust their lives to live more like a husband and wife or else split. Her response was, "You can't tell me what to do." At his insistence, she found a separate place to live, and several months later they were divorced.

When Lissie first spoke with Brian after it became clear he was divorcing, she focused only on what he should do. She told him, "Brian, I know that Janie didn't take her wedding vows as seriously as you did, and you're the more loyal of the two. But God gave us His restrictions about divorce for a reason. You should have stayed with her in order to maintain a Christian witness." Brian protested that Janie had told him she was "Christian enough" and she just wanted Brian to let her conduct her life as she saw fit. That, Brian told his sister, was not acceptable to him.

After several futile discussions, the siblings still could not agree about what was really best for Brian. Their differing perspectives only chilled their relationship. As much as he tried to convince Lissie that he had made the right decision, he knew she'd never support him.

Two years later, Brian went to visit his parents, unaware that Lissie had also dropped in to see them. When he entered, he noticed that his sister was red-eyed, clearly from crying. He learned that her husband had told her the night before that he was leaving her; she strongly suspected another woman. As she poured out her story, Brian could see that Lissie was thinking more deeply about herself than ever before. Lissie put her hand on Brian's arm and said, "I need to ask for your forgiveness for the way I shunned you when you and Janie split. I was so focused on why it happened that I neglected to notice how much pain you were in. I'm just now beginning to realize that we all have feet of clay; none of us is immune from problems. You didn't need me to scrutinize your motives; instead, you needed someone to share in your humanness."

Only those who are aware of their ongoing need for grace are able to look for opportunities to extend grace to those who fall short. Lissie's ability to bond with her brother grew in proportion to her own admission of vulnerability. As she had to admit that her own life could derail, the stringent beliefs that guided her gave way to a recognition that Christianity is best evidenced where love takes precedence over correctness.

Grace Requires Brokenness

As Daniel was trying to make sense of how he had been received well by some Christians and poorly by others, he made an interesting observation: "I've found that the people who have either been divorced or had major personal setbacks are the ones who are most likely to be kind to me. As a general rule, the ones who are most pious and condescending have not suffered as many personal losses. It's like their clean personal résumé predisposes them to look down upon failures like me."

Second only to Jesus, the apostle Paul was a powerful pioneer in moving the New Testament church away from legalism and toward grace. Repeatedly he reminded Christians of the far-reaching nature of God's love for us:

- "We have peace with God through our Lord Jesus Christ, through whom also we have obtained our introduction by faith into this grace in which we stand; and we exult in the hope of the glory of God" (Romans 5:1–2).
- "For I am convinced that neither death nor life, nor angels nor principalities, nor things present nor things to come, nor powers, nor height, nor depth, nor any other created thing shall be able to separate us from the love of God which is in Christ Jesus our Lord" (Romans 8:38–39).
- "In Him we have redemption through His blood, the forgiveness of our trespasses, according to the riches of His grace, which He lavished upon us" (Ephesians 1:7–8).

Let's keep in mind that prior to becoming a Christian Paul received today's equivalent of a Ph.D. in theology. He knew scripture backward and forward. He had a brilliant mind. His communication skills were keen. Despite his brilliance, he had not yet known grace.

There was one thing that caused Paul to understand the enormousness of grace: brokenness. You know his story of salvation on the road to Damascus. Blinded, he was befriended by Ananias, though Christian friends had warned him not to go near this man who had persecuted the church. Galatians 1:17 reveals that after his conversion he made his way to Arabia, probably to reflect on the new direction his life would take. He let the Holy Spirit reveal to him how the Old Testament teaching was fulfilled in Jesus, and he probably began pulling together ideas that would become foundational for his later teachings. During the years after his salvation and before his missionary journeys, it is highly probable that Paul went through a soul searching of the kind that few have ever experienced before.

Perhaps he asked himself questions of this kind: Why have I been so full of hate? What is it about me that makes me want to destroy people who disagree with me? Do I even know the nature of love, much less how to give it away? What will it take to get followers of Christ to know that my priorities are now right? How can I possibly make restitution toward the people I have so deeply hurt?

Many years later, in his well-known "thorn in the flesh" passage, Paul told his readers that in the past he had reason to boast, but through his encounter with Christ he now realized that all such boasting was empty. The Lord allowed him to sustain an ongoing burden, his thorn in the flesh, to remind him of the humility that was so necessary to remain as God's model. He pleaded with God to remove this burden, until God revealed to him, "My grace is sufficient for you, for power is perfected in weakness" (II Corinthians 12:9). Paul then went on to claim that if he ever boasted again, it would be about his weaknesses.

In today's lingo, Paul's message could be restated: "If you want to grow as a Christian, weakness is where it's at, man."

Daniel, divorced after a twenty-five-year marriage, told me in no uncertain terms that this teaching from Paul's writing was undoubtedly the most difficult for him to digest: "I never thought of brokenness as something that would be good for me. From the days of my youth, I've concentrated on being the best, making straight

As, being the leader, keeping a right reputation. Even as a Christian, I continued in that same vein of thought. I was pleased with myself when I was selected as a deacon. I liked being on the important church committees. It was vital to me that others held me in high regard. I really worked on my reputation for goodness.

"But now look at me," he said. "Though all those good things about my past are still true, everything about me is interpreted differently as soon as someone learns that I'm a divorcee. I'm just not accustomed to being associated with failure."

A couple of years after his divorce, I encountered Daniel after not seeing him for some time. When I asked how his new life was unfolding, he replied, "There is one *very* interesting by-product of my being a divorcee. I feel a capacity to love people now in ways that I never knew before." He explained to me that he had a new appreciation for what it is like to need an arm around the shoulder from someone who can gently say, "I'm pulling for you." He had also learned a new path to freedom by admitting his humanness, as opposed to trying to appear superhuman: "It is odd to say this, but being forced to go public with my brokenness was the best thing that could have happened to me. I've learned how to love on a much deeper level."

Grace Can Be Misconstrued as License

Years ago, I had a penetrating discussion with a pastor friend who admitted that he sometimes felt paralyzed when faced with the situation of a newly discovered divorce in his congregation. "I'm caught between two conflicting responses," he said to me. "Having spoken to many people who are getting divorced, I know that it can be an incredibly agonizing experience. It is a time of great insecurity for that person; I know love and kindness are qualities they need greatly." Pausing, he shook his head and continued, "My role as pastor carries an aura of authority, and people gauge my positions on every subject very carefully. If it becomes known that I am too kind to a divorcee, there is a 100 percent guarantee that I'll be criticized by someone who wants me to arm-twist the divorcing parties rather than accept them."

It is true that some people exiting a marriage do so in a lax fashion, with shallow reasons for ending the relationship. I recall one man who began an affair, which then led to the dissolution of his marriage. He had two young children and a wife who made it clear that she wanted to preserve the union, but he left them nonetheless because (in his own words) he "didn't like the restrictions" of family life. This man would offer an easy smile as he referred to his circumstances, looking straight at me with a smug grin. "I know that God's grace can cover all sins! Even though divorce is not desirable, God is so good to smile on me and smother me in His arms." Lost in his glee over God's grace was any hint of sadness or brokenness over the collapse of his family structure.

Sometimes, shallow people who are committed to a life of sheer self-gratification latch onto the message of God's grace and run with it as if it can be interpreted as total permission to live any way they want. They overemphasize that God's character is predisposed to be kind and forgiving. Bypassing guilt, which can rightly stimulate each of us to go before God with a willingness to honestly make restitution for wrongs, these people quickly pronounce themselves spiritually whole, having virtually no comprehension of the shallowness that guides their lives.

So how can we proceed when we witness some people interpreting grace as license for irresponsibility? Confrontation is an option, though in many cases it may not lead to the desired insights. My personal tendency is at least to address the seriousness of the subject when I am face to face with such blatant grace abuse. For instance, when this man spoke to me as he did, I told him it would be wise to take time apart from his new and fun life to contemplate the direction in which he was headed. I expressed concern that he had moved too hurriedly to end his marriage in order to pursue this new woman. His reply was predictable: "Well, no one really understands that actually I spent years working hard to improve my marriage.

I honestly feel like I gave it a good effort, but to people looking at my life from the outside, it could appear that I made a sudden decision when I really didn't." This man was never receptive to any input that might dissuade him from his decision.

If it seems apparent that some receive grace in a shallow fashion, Christians may conclude, "I don't want any part in encouraging people to be loose regarding God's truth about grace." This is understandable. There may even be times when Christians rightly put distance between themselves and those who abuse grace because they do not want to condone a wrong lifestyle.

Let's affirm, though, that although some may grab onto grace as an excuse for selfishness, it does not require an all-or-nothing response. "Since some people may misapply grace," the reasoning might go, "I don't want to be too liberal in my endorsement of grace." To hold back in giving grace because it might be misapplied is to allow your Christian walk to be monitored by sinful influences, not a godly pull.

In an interesting parable recorded in Matthew 13:24–30, Jesus compared the kingdom of God to a wheat field. Good seed was sowed in the ground, but at night the enemy mixed in tares (weeds) among the wheat. Only at the time of harvest was it fully realized that the bad was mixed in with the good. The parable ends with the landowner instructing his workers to allow both to grow together until harvest time, when they can be separated.

Christians do not need their willingness to extend grace to be spoiled by the possibility that some of it may be received by manipulators. The alternative is to withhold it from all who might need it. Though grace would then not be misapplied by crooked people, neither would it be received by those in genuine need of it.

My discussion with the pastor who was reluctant to be too free in being kind to divorcees ended with his stating: "Divorce is almost always a touchy subject because people tend to pick sides with one spouse or the other. That puts me in a no-win situation because if I'm open to one side the other will feel slighted. Frankly, the easiest thing for me to do is stay low-profile when these circumstances arise."

People like Gwen and Daniel learn to draw strength from God when human conduits for grace decide against the low-profile approach. They come to recognize grace for what it is: a radical communication of love that is so focused on the recipient's need for it that self-protection is not an issue. Grace is a pure gift reflecting the depth of God's yearning to draw imperfect people to Him.

Chapter Eight

The Perils of Imperative Thinking

Recall Michelle, the divorcing mother from Chapter One who was coming to the end of her twenty-three-year marriage. The relationship with her husband, Allen, was typified by verbal haranguing, spitting, shoving, rages, and chronic anger. Michelle tried to explain to her pastor that she could no longer allow herself and her children to be exposed to the indignities of this type of treatment. At this point, the pastor told her that although he sympathized with her difficult life, he could not endorse her decision because Allen had not committed adultery.

Sitting before me in my counseling office, Michelle wore a weary look of defeat. Her eyes were puffy and her countenance was drawn. Heaving a great sigh and with tears in her eyes, she spoke: "I don't know what more I could do to satisfy my critics so they would know that I've given the marriage my best effort. My pastor *did* concede that a temporary separation might be in order, so I tried that and things only got worse. Allen cut off all the money, and each time we tried to talk it was only a matter of minutes before he'd be screaming and cursing at me. My poor kids have such a marred image of how a man should treat a woman that I'm afraid they'll be scarred for life."

Her voice became increasingly tense as she continued. "I was forced to talk to a lawyer because he would not cooperate with my need to take care of the household bills during our separation. We filed a divorce petition and finally got him to agree to a monthly amount for the bare necessities. Of course, he was infuriated, and his rages have worsened. If he thinks he can win me back by intimidation, he's missed the boat. The kids are so fed up with him;

they won't see him at all. My youngest, the eleven-year-old, went with him to the movies one Saturday, but he said he'll never do it again because he just harassed him about our separation. I'm telling you, he's gone crazy!"

Michelle agonized over her past, wondering how her marriage could have deteriorated so much. "When we first met, I knew he was a strongly opinionated, religious person, even to the extent of being self-righteous. I had been brought up very conservatively, so even though I thought he was a little overzealous at times, I didn't think much of it because I believed that Christians *should* have strong convictions. At the time, being dogmatic didn't seem so wrong, but as the years have passed I've determined that being correct and insisting on doctrinal accuracy has its downside. It was Allen's sense of correctness that triggered his rages. And, you know, I've been thinking, it was Pastor James's need for correctness that caused him to be so unbending about divorce even after he conceded that I was in a very ungodly mess."

Trying to help her put this in perspective, I explained, "Michelle, you have had a lot of exposure to what I call *imperative thinking*." Though she was unsure of my terminology, I could tell that this struck a chord with her, so I explained further. "You may recall from your grade school days that an imperative sentence is direct and demanding. When we say something is imperative, there usually is an urgent command that has to be acknowledged. In our vocabulary we have a lot of imperative words: *have to, must, can't, should, supposed to, got to, need to, had better,* and others.

As I was speaking, Michelle nodded. "That's exactly the way things have been communicated in our house since the beginning. I've had the feeling that there is a mold I'm supposed to fit. If I ever differ from Allen, then I'm to be chastised until I can agree that his way is the only way things can be done. He's constantly focused on what's *supposed to* be done or how I've *got to* act and feel."

Nodding, I replied: "That's the essence of imperative thinking. When someone is being imperative, he or she acts as if life consists of a long list of duties and obligations. The goal becomes to conform life to that list." Michelle was in full agreement as I spoke. "My sense is that for years Allen has had an agenda for you, and he has made it his self-appointed task to make sure you stick to that agenda. Does that sound familiar?"

Again Michelle nodded as she described a couple of instances when Allen insisted that she *had to* have the same priorities as he did. He wanted her to discipline the kids correctly (translated: his way), he wanted her to spend money only as he determined, and he insisted that she arrange her schedule to suit his desires. When she failed to meet the agenda, the result was anger, often in the form of wild rage.

Michelle and I discussed how imperative thinking was also at the root of the mind-set that she encountered from the people who insisted her divorce did not unfold properly. These people were taking the perfect principles from scripture and turning them into imperative, nonnegotiable musts and have tos. As far as her critics were concerned, it became their obligation to keep people like Michelle in line. They insisted that she follow the agenda they prescribed, even if it meant forgoing any discernment or common sense. Often their intentions were honorable, but their insistence upon correctness kept them from appreciating the emotional trauma she experienced. Imperative thinking prevented them from empathizing with the indignity of her home atmosphere. Because they were so busy trying to get her to follow the rules, they inadvertently wounded her even more in her recovery process.

As Michelle grasped the nature of imperative thinking, she acknowledged: "I can think of many times when *I've* been just as imperative as anyone else. Sometimes my imperative thinking causes me to focus on the ways I think others had better behave or respond. I can be critical." Then shifting gears, she recognized: "Also, I can be quite imperative in my own self-directed thoughts. I'm constantly worrying about how I'm supposed to act or how I should have handled myself. The reason I become so consumed with the imperative ideas of others is because I put such a heavy requirement on myself to be correct." I really appreciated Michelle's self-honesty.

The Origins of Imperative Thinking

There is something seductive about imperative thinking that keeps sincere people returning to it repeatedly. About 99 percent of the time a person has an imperative thought, there is a strong element of correctness associated with it. For instance, if someone says "You *ought to be* forgiving," it's hard to argue against that. If another states, "Couples *should* learn how to argue fairly so their anger won't get out of hand," it is absurd to refute such a notion. Imperative thinking is strongly anchored in order and correctness—and therein lies its problem. Does this seem strange?

Recall our earlier discussion (from Chapter Two) about Adam and Eve's fall into sin. Adam had been told that he could not eat of the Tree of Knowledge of Good and Evil because God, and only God, was fit to determine all the elements of right and wrong. Humanity was given the gift of freedom, which is defined as the privilege of choices, but it would be in their vested interest to refrain from that Tree. Symbolically, the message was, "You have your freedom, but it is wisest to choose to submit to God's standard of right and wrong. Don't complicate things by making up your own standards too."

Recall that when Satan tempted Adam and Eve to eat of the Tree, his hook was "and you will be as God." Taking of the Tree's fruit represented humanity's attempt to exert godlike control over life. At the moment they did so, false pride became indigenous to human nature; the "language" of false pride became imperative thinking. Adam had decided, "I'll be in charge now and I'll decide what is right and what is wrong." He wanted to be absolute, meaning that all he said would have full authority and force.

Throughout time, as humans attempted to be in charge or to insist on a code of correctness, they have displayed Adam's imperative thinking style. As an inherent part of our sin nature, imperative thinking is natural to everyone. Each of us can be arrogant enough to assume that we know how events are supposed to unfold. We are naturally inclined to think, "You must," or "I ought to," or "You're supposed to."

Christians may sometimes veil their own imperative agenda by appealing to scripture (*"I'm* not saying you're supposed to live this way; *the Bible* says that's how you've got live"). Christians can rationalize that they are merely remaining true to scripture when they insist on maintaining their imperatives. Honesty, however, requires that they admit their biblical imperatives are nonetheless intended to fit life into a neatly prescribed box. With their life inside the secure parameters of their imperative thinking, they maintain their own comfort. Invariably, imperative thinking is linked to self-centeredness.

The subject of divorce, being such a high-stakes issue, readily arouses imperative thinking in the minds of those trying to make sense of it. Almost everyone correctly assumes that marriage is the preferred choice over divorce. Common sense, if nothing else, indicates that it is best for a family to remain intact if at all feasible. Knowing this, when we hear of a couple divorcing our natural inclination is to say, "But you shouldn't," or "You can't." Such a reaction reflects our high regard for marriage, yet in the meantime it denies free will.

When I talk with people about the misguided aspects of imperative thinking, I point out that this mind-set is control-based. Then I explain two fundamental beliefs that guide me as I try to make sense of the things of the world: control is an illusion, and freedom is reality.

Imperative thinkers are kidding themselves when they assume they can or should control the decisions of others. Their communication often becomes coercive or invasive as they attempt to force struggling people to do what is right. In doing so, they forget that God allows each person to exercise free will. He gives His perfect principles, and then He lets individuals choose how they will manage those principles. No human can control how another human will respond to God's principles.

Sinful pride, however, can inhibit us from recognizing and acknowledging the limits of our ability to control others. When one Christian insists that another Christian should make specific choices, this is denying the reality of free will. It is appropriate that we confront, teach, and exhort one another, but it is also necessary to remember that it is impossible to control another person.

Michelle explained to me: "I was raised in a conservative home where there was a very strong sense of right and wrong. When I had to make a decision, I was specifically told what it had better be. Choices weren't a big part of our discussions, particularly when major issues were on the line. As I got to know Allen in my twenties, I saw he was poured out of the same mold as my parents. Right was right and there was no room for negotiation. Although I sometimes disliked being so fixed on what *had to* be done, that's the way I had been taught to think, so I went along with it. I asked no questions."

She continued reflecting out loud about the effects of imperative thinking. "The older I've become, the less convinced I am that you can fit every decision into a hard black-or-white box. Life just isn't that cut and dried. I *know* a lot of Allen's commands were off base, *way* off base. He'd insist, for instance, that I had to discipline the kids more firmly, and if I didn't he'd step in with harsh words toward them and toward me. He *always* felt like he was right; to him being right was the only thing that mattered. In the meantime, I'd watch our family life deteriorate all around us. When I'd call this into question, it would make no difference. He just *had* to be in control, and in the end our family life went way out of control."

Then Michelle added: "Once our church friends found out about our separation, I was stunned by the need that some folks had to keep me in line. I was trying to get away from this ultracontrolling husband, and then I came face to face with controlling Christians. I am terribly disillusioned by the whole experience."

Controlling people seemingly have sole proprietorship of correctness and are propelled to impose their convictions on others, but there are elements at work that can be destructive, or at least contradictory to God's method of influencing people. Let's explore this further.

Knowledge Makes You Arrogant

At first glance, it seems preposterous to assume that knowledge can be a bad thing. After all, isn't it the people with the most knowledge who become the leaders, the movers and shakers? Knowledge is power. Knowledge impresses others. Knowledge leads to solutions. What's so wrong about that?

In my personal life, great emphasis was placed on the necessity of being well educated. Both of my parents have advanced degrees, my father having earned a doctorate and my mother a master's degree. Very early in college, I determined to stick with school through my doctorate; my brother did the same. Clearly, I have lived with the assumption that knowledge propels a person to the right places.

That stated, I find it fascinating as I examine humanity's beginnings in Eden to consider that the one restraint placed upon Adam and Eve was in eating from the Tree of Knowledge—specifically, the knowledge of good and evil. What could possibly be so bad in knowing about good and evil?

God knew that once humans assumed knowledge, it could easily be accompanied by a sense of self-importance. In fact, this self-important attitude could cause people to lord it over others who might not be so enlightened. To get an idea of how this works, think of a time when you were convinced you were right and others in your presence were wrong. What did it do to your attitude? Were you critical? annoyed? impatient? smug? condescending? Surely you have had times when the dark side of knowledge led you into negativity.

When Paul wrote to the Corinthians about their many problems and disagreements, he wanted to do more than just resolve disputes. He answered questions (as we explored in Chapter Five) about such matters as divorce or eating meat offered to idols, but in doing so he also sought to expose potential problems that accompanied their attempts to establish correct response.

In chapter 8 (just following his statements about divorce), Paul begins, "We know that we all have knowledge. Knowledge makes arrogance, but love edifies." In essence, he admits that all are capable of formulating their own opinions. However, in our clinging to strong opinions, the problem of arrogance can easily arise. Being of a right opinion can "permit" us to act disrespectfully toward others— and that's not desirable.

Divorce is a subject that arouses myriad opinionated responses. Virtually all of us have seen how divorce can bring out the worst in some personalities. It can confuse children, who through no fault of their own have to endure major adjustments in lifestyle. We have witnessed the financial hardships caused by divorce, and we have noticed that divorce can motivate individuals to rationalize selfishness in a variety of creative ways. As observers of the strains caused by divorce, we then find it is easy to spew out strong opinions each time we know of another couple who have gone to the marriage graveyard.

It *is* good to hold opinions that testify to the positive aspects of marriage. In an age when divorce is often sought for flippant reasons and marriage is viewed as easily discarded, it is right for us to stand up for the traditional values that are so essential for family cohesion. I have no problem with those who openly emphasize the need for higher respect for the institution of marriage. In fact, I grieve when I learn of people who shrug off the notion of easy divorce as an inevitability that we just have to accept.

Those who hold strong convictions about marriage and divorce need to exercise care, though. Their opinions do not give them the right to be condescending to those who have missed the mark. Michelle told me, "Once the news about my divorce spread among the people I knew at church, I felt like a marked woman. Don't get me wrong; some people were very nice to me and offered words of consolation." Shaking her head, she went on: "But some people were just downright rude to me. There was one woman in particular, whom I had known casually for several years, who clearly ignored me several times when I saw her around the church. Finally, I had a chance to stop her and ask if there was anything wrong, and if something had come between us that I needed to know about. She very quickly became flustered and told me that she was having a hard time with my divorce. It bothered her that a person could be divorced and yet act like everything was just fine in their lives. I assured her that this had not been an overnight decision. I also explained that, while I was doing my best to hang in there, this was the most difficult trauma I had experienced."

"So did your talk with her ease the tension between the two of you?"

"No, not at all. She told me we'd have to finish our talk later, and she left. She just went back to ignoring me, and I've decided not to push the issue."

This flustered woman was displaying a mind-set common to imperative people: "You just don't measure up." Apparently she had staked out her ground regarding opinions about marriage and divorce and had decided she could only fellowship with those who met her standard. Her downfall was in requiring others to think as she did in order to be her friend.

Contrast this thinking with the mind of Christ. Remember that Jesus embodied the mind of God. If anyone held a powerful belief in His own correctness, it had to be Jesus. Yet despite His high opinions, one of the descriptions given to Him was "a friend of sinners" (Matthew 11:19). Would Jesus expect anything less from His current representatives?

Pray that we will never be so knowledgeable that we feel permitted to be condescending toward others who do not meet our interpretation of the standard.

Imperative Thinking Inhibits Love

Following closely on the heels of condescending communication, imperative thinkers find it difficult to love fully. Anyone can love someone who happens to meet his or her criteria for success, but it takes a person with maturity to love someone who is outside the mold. In evangelical mainstream Christianity, divorce is definitely a subject outside the mold. Many with an imperative mind-set find it hard to love divorcees as fully as they might love individuals with a thriving marriage.

Michelle spoke candidly with me about her run-ins with Christians who insisted that she should live according to their agendas. "I've had people telling me how I'm supposed to conduct my life now that I'm newly single, and it's driving me nuts!"

"What are you being told that you must do?"

"I have one friend who is constantly cautioning me about how to conduct myself with men. She seems to think that I'll be a weak pushover who will have an impossible time setting boundaries. If she hears that I've had a friendly conversation with a man, she jumps all over it and tells me that I've got to wait before getting involved. She's worried that I will let my kids see me getting attached to a guy. She's making all sorts of assumptions that are off-base because, first of all, I have no interest in dating, period. Even if I did, it's not her place to tell me how to do it. I'm a grown woman, and I'm capable of making my own decisions. I don't understand why she feels the need to give me advice that I don't ask for."

"What is it," I asked, "about this unsolicited advice that turns you off the most?"

"It's plain and simple," she replied. "When I feel that someone like this friend is telling me how to live my life, I'm hearing information that's probably good for me, yet there is one huge ingredient missing: Love."

Indeed, she hit the nail on the head. It is certainly good to know God's perfect will regarding lifestyle choices and priorities, but love supersedes all. When we humans attempt to impose imperatives onto others, we run the risk of misrepresenting God. Our notion is not necessarily off the mark, but our imperatives can send messages contradictory to love.

Whenever we communicate with one another, we send two types of messages, one overt and the other covert. The overt message is the spoken word, while the covert message is the unspoken innuendo. When one Christian imperatively tells another "Here is how you must live your life," the overt message may have a ring of truth to it. For instance, Michelle's friend was probably right in what she had to say about being slow to get involved with another man. However, the covert message can be one of nonacceptance, distrust, or disapproval.

Every communication is accompanied by a host of nonverbal cues. They range from tone of voice to facial expressions, to hand gestures, and more. Whenever we speak to each other, it is often the covert messages that have the greater impact. As a simple example, suppose you and a friend are in public observing a young couple holding hands and speaking fondly to each other. Your friend says, "Isn't that special?" How do you react to this simple statement? It all depends on the delivery. If the words are spoken softly and are accompanied by a pleasant smile, you will probably respond with a similar gentle reaction. If, however, the words are accompanied by a sarcastic tone and a facial scowl, your reaction will be less enthusiastic. Words have far less impact in communication than the attitude in how the words are spoken.

Imperative people tend to be so focused on the correctness of their words that they are oblivious to the way they covertly communicate unlovingly. A minister once told me, "If anyone in my care starts treating God's principles lightly, I'll be all over them in a flash." As you might imagine, his voice was sharp and his lips were drawn tight in sternness. My own immediate internal reaction was, "I'd hate to be in his care." Why? His covert message told me that it was more important for him to control people than to love them.

Christ's message was the opposite. It was more important for Him to first establish love. Self-control would eventually follow. As an example of this mind-set, He told a parable that is recorded in John 10:1–5. Sheep inside a pen will not respond well to a thief trying to take them captive. Instead, their shepherd has much greater success in leading the sheep when he enters the door, calls them by name, and then leads them into the open field.

His analogy was meant to underscore how individuals follow leaders who attempt to exert influence not by force or manipulation but by relationships. Christ calls His own by name. He knows each of His flock, and His flock knows Him as a caring guide. We in His flock do not follow Him because of His use of force, but because we are attracted to His kind and gentle ways.

Imperative people find it difficult to be tender to those who are hurting or who are outside the mold because they insist that life should fit into neat slots. Emotional needs, character flaws, or off-base circumstances do not fit neatly into those slots, which means those who don't fit are rejected. This mind-set reduces imperative people to those who can love only if the right conditions are met. Because God's love is not conditional, it follows that the imperative person's "love" is simply not love at all.

Michelle summarized her needs well when she told me: "I know that there are some people who don't understand why I'm divorced, and maybe they never will. I'm not asking for anyone to condone what they don't understand, but I'm guessing they have imperfections too. All I'm asking for is the same kindness that they would want and need if their imperfections become known. There is no way any of us will measure up all the time."

Ultimately, Imperative Thinking Is Evil

Evil is a strong word, one not to be used lightly. When I suggest that imperative thinking can ultimately become evil, understand that I am not suggesting that every person who has ever had an imperative thought is evil. (This would include all of us.) What I am saying is that if we indulge an imperative mind-set we need to realize that this pattern of thinking is exactly the way Satan wants Christians to respond. He wants us to think in terms of control, power, and dominance.

Recall Satan's original temptation to Adam and Eve: eat of the Tree of Knowledge of Good and Evil and you will be as God. The original scheme Satan used to draw humanity away from God was the temptation to be in control. This is precisely what God did not want. God wants no humans to take upon themselves the task of ultimately forcing people to do right and refrain from wrong. He Himself refrains from this use of His power. Certainly there are times when it is appropriate to counsel, teach, or confront. There are moments when it is right to establish consequences or set boundaries for people in perpetual sin. But ultimately there is only one God, only one Holy Spirit, and it isn't *me*—or you.

People who habitually relate to others with imperative thinking leading the way are attempting to exert control over others that is not theirs to exert. Even though it is good to openly discuss beliefs about doctrine or lifestyle priorities, it is ultimately the task of the Holy Spirit to bring conviction to others. The work of the Holy Spirit is often hindered when humans press too powerfully with their need to control.

A man whom we'll call Greg left his wife, Ellen, and was dating a woman named Cheryl. He came to me because he was having major misgivings about this new relationship. He wanted help as he tried to determine the best way to proceed in this new relationship. As is my usual custom, I wanted to gain a perspective of the broader picture, so I asked him to talk with me about Cheryl and why he left his wife. He told me that for years his and Ellen's communication had deteriorated, and they no longer wanted to spend time together. That is not necessarily a good reason to leave a marriage, but it is nonetheless what he did. I learned that Greg had a deep history of avoiding conflicts. He tended to carry frustration inside without expressing it outwardly.

The longer I talked with Greg, the more I sensed that his marriage was salvageable. He told me Ellen probably would have come to counseling, but he bolted before giving it a chance. Even now, he surmised that if he gave up his rebellion and sought Ellen out, she would be willing to discuss the possibility of reconciliation. Learning this, I asked, "So what is hindering you from at least trying to make amends with Ellen?"

Shaking his head, Greg told me: "Just a couple of weeks after I moved into my apartment, two men from my church paid me a visit to discuss my marriage. Understand that it's very unnatural for me to reveal my feelings, but I decided to give it a shot and explain why I had felt so disgruntled. The more I talked to those guys, the more apparent it was that they had come expecting to reform me on the spot. Any past hurt or disappointment I disclosed to them was immediately met with some form of rebuttal. Before long they were speaking coercively with me, telling me that I was a sinner and I'd better get my life right with God. By the time they finally left there was a tremendous tension among us. I was so angry I couldn't sleep all night."

Greg's visitors had approached him with the intent of getting him to see the wrong of his ways. They were correct to recognize that he was using questionable judgment, and it was noble that they would care enough to address the issue with him. Their approach, however, left much to be desired. They were so imperative in their delivery ("You *must* repent *now*") that any evidence of kindness or concern was completely lost. The net result was that Greg, who was initially receptive, felt more alienated from the Christian message after they left.

Once people commit their lives to Christ, Satan does not cease from exerting his own negative influences. Within Christian circles, perhaps the greatest evidence of his influence is imperative thinking, which translates into a judgmental spirit. When Christians attempt to force the correct agenda onto others, they are living in consistency with Satan's first temptation to humanity: take ultimate knowledge upon yourself and try to play God. It did not succeed with Adam and Eve, and it will not work with people like Greg's visitors. When imperative ideas are imposed, even though the gist of the message may be correct, the deeper, covert message is one of condemnation, or rejection, or conditional acceptance.

Jesus spoke the well-known words of John 3:16 to Nicodemus, explaining God's love for the world that propelled Him to send Christ for salvation. He followed this declaration with the explanation, "For God did not send the Son into the world to condemn the world, but that the world through Him might be saved" (John 3:17). Jesus' approach to drawing people to Him was anchored in love, not condemnation. Someone like Greg, for instance, can often be open to receive godly counsel when God's emissaries show themselves to be patient, understanding, and kind.

At its farthest extreme, an attempt to communicate truth in a controlling fashion is destructive in the sense that it inhibits the presence of God's love. As a contrast, when people like Greg or Michelle are lovingly encouraged to consider godly counsel, they are more likely to be receptive to it. Truth can be most readily absorbed if it is presented in a way that acknowledges respect for freedom of choice, without coercion or obligation. God's truth is so innately reasonable and appealing that if anyone has a genuine desire to receive it, demands or force are unnecessary.

When people have the pain of divorce upon them, the last thing they need is an iron-fisted command to get marriage right. Already in a state of regret, embarrassment, or frustration, they are more in need of acceptance. Poor choices may need to be discussed or priorities rearranged, but before these people can be receptive to input they first want to know, "Do you care?" A controlling agenda has pushed many a hurting person away from the Lord's truth. Kindness and patience, on the other hand, can be the beginning of a deeper delving into the experience of a life yielded to God.

In the next chapter, we explore several alternatives to imperative thinking as we consider how to respond to divorcees in the most helpful manner.

Chapter Nine

What Divorcees Need

Sitting in the living area of his new apartment, Kyle was killing time watching television. "My life sure has become dull in the last six months," he mused to himself. For years, he would go home to a beehive of busyness with his wife and two daughters. They each had numerous involvements in civic, school, or church activities. Kyle was the kind of dad who enjoyed helping his girls through tough chemistry homework, and before either of them could drive he took his turn getting them to and from their many activities. Now his younger daughter was enrolled in the local community college while the other was three hours away at college. He and his former wife had known the day would probably come when they would separate. Now, sure enough, he was Mr. Single in his early fifties, wondering how he would start anew at this late time in his life. "I'm too old," he told himself, "to be worried about getting dates or trying to determine who I want to be." Feeling out of touch with people was definitely not the norm for him, and for the first time in his life he knew what it was like to feel depressed. Hopefulness and optimism eluded him.

The phone rang, and he was surprised to hear from an old friend. "Hey, Kyle, it's Suzie," came the animated voice on the other end. Kyle had first met Suzie and her husband, Ron, twenty years before. It had been a couple of years since they last talked, but they had the kind of relationship where they could pick it up without skipping a beat. "I just heard from a friend about your divorce. I wish I had known sooner because Ron and I would have liked to help in any way we could."

The two talked for a while as Kyle told his old friend about his new life, and then Suzie chimed in. "You're just going to have to come over for dinner." Kyle's social life wasn't exactly booming, so he welcomed the opportunity to get out for an evening. They set up a time; as they hung up, Kyle felt especially pleased that someone would care enough to initiate this kind of contact. He reflected, "I never realized how much I needed my friends. I never knew that I'd have such an awkward time getting over my loneliness."

Immediately, when Kyle arrived at his friends' home, he felt at ease. They exchanged the typical updates regarding life's highlights since they had last seen each other. Kyle was eager to hear of their daughter, who was the same age as his older child. They recalled fun times when the families spent weekends together. Laughing, they reminisced about how Ron somehow hooked Kyle's daughter in the ear years ago with a fishing lure. They recalled old friends that neither had heard from. They reminisced about the pleasant times shared with other couples who, like themselves, had struggled just to make ends meet in the days when they had little ones.

Finally, after dinner, Suzie shifted gears as she began talking about Kyle's most recent turn of events. "I was very sorry to hear about your split with Vickie, but I can't really say I was surprised."

Kyle had heard others say similar words, but he wanted Suzie's perspective, so he asked, "What signals did you pick up that led you to think we might be in trouble?"

"Well, I knew that you had always been a people person. You liked to connect with your friends in ways that Vickie did not. I could also tell that you two weren't on the same wavelength when you would share something personal. She always seemed a bit uncomfortable if you revealed very much about your needs or feelings, and I could sense that it caused tension between the two of you." Kyle nodded knowingly as he thought it amazing that Suzie was so perceptive. "I also noticed," she continued, "in the last few times we saw you together that you seemed to be holding onto a quiet frustration. Bitterness might be too strong a word, but I knew that behind your mask something wasn't right."

Kyle was relieved that Suzie and Ron showed such willingness to talk on a personal level. They continued to discuss some of the problems that led to his divorce from Vickie, but the bulk of their attention was given to Kyle's current struggle to restructure his life and redefine himself. He explained, "For close to thirty years my identity was as a family man, not some swinging single. I've known for a long time that my marriage could end like this, but I still was not emotionally prepared to handle all the changes that are before me."

As he continued to talk with his friends, he explained how his social life had changed significantly. Before, it revolved around the couples he knew. "Now I feel like a fifth wheel in lots of settings, so it's easier for me just to bow out." Friends encouraged him to date but he just wasn't ready yet to face that potential.

"On another front," Kyle revealed, "things were changing anyway; I'm referring to my relationship with my daughters. One is a freshman in college, and the other is applying to graduate school. It's like I'm in the middle of a double whammy. My kids are out of the coop, making me an empty-nester, and I'm now single and trying to figure out what it is that a middle-aged single guy is supposed to do. Nothing feels normal right now."

Kyle is typical of many people who have experienced divorce. His identity was long anchored in his role as husband and father. For years, he was known as Vicki's husband. He was known to the community at large as a nice, friendly guy who went home every night to typical suburban home life. Now, though, as a divorcee people were not so sure how to interpret him. "We thought he was a good family guy," the reasoning might go, "but obviously there must be something about him that we didn't really know. Hmmm. I wonder if he's really the kind of person we thought he was."

Kyle told his friends, "I feel like I ought to stand up on a rooftop and shout to anyone who might care to listen: 'Hey, I'm still an OK guy! I promise!' But I don't suppose that would really do any good, would it?"

Like many in his position, he felt self-conscious about his damaged identity. Though he had been a secure man most of his life, he realized that some personal, hidden insecurities were surfacing now. He wanted and needed affirmation from family and friends; at the same time, he did not want to appear weak or needy. All sorts of conflicting emotions floated around in his personality as he felt his way into a new life. He was dealing at new levels with embarrassment, relief, loneliness, calm, guilt, anger, hopefulness, uncertainty, caution, eagerness, and confusion.

Speaking to Ron and Suzie, he explained. "You've known me long enough to know that I'm not normally emotionally conflicted. I've never been the hand-wringing type of person who wastes time worrying. But I've got to admit, it's been a challenge for me to realize just how many emotions I'm capable of. I can tell that I'm not really settled right now!"

Bearing Burdens

People in transition such as Kyle need friends like Suzie and Ron to help keep them anchored in reality. Though ultimately it is each individual's sole responsibility to chart a course for healthy living, loving friends can certainly make the journey less bumpy. Galatians 6:2 instructs, "Bear one another's burdens and thus fulfill the law of Christ."

In previous chapters, we have seen how divorcees undergo plenty of scrutiny, often accompanied by judgment, skepticism, or rejection. The body of Christ, however—even as we maintain principles about marital commitments and godly virtues—is generous in offering hope and kindness to those who are the most devastated. Through my counseling practice and my own acquaintances, I have witnessed how easy it is for divorcees to lose their focus on Christian values because few people (sometimes no one) were willing to come along beside them and offer assistance.

The aftermath of a divorce is an excellent opportunity for hurting individuals to experience tremendous spiritual growth. Many people have a heightened readiness to seek God when the chips are down. Conversely, this is also a time when individuals can feel especially inadequate, and when little assistance is forthcoming they begin to flounder spiritually, perhaps succumbing to behaviors and temptations not familiar to them during their marriage. The body of Christ shows itself, therefore, to be most mature not by loving and guiding only those who already fit the bill but by ministering to those who feel the most disenfranchised. This is an opportunity to consider divorcees as seekers looking for reasons to hope, not people deserving scorn or second-class treatment.

There are several key qualities that can be offered as gifts to divorcees as you minister to and interact with them through their transition process. Let's examine some of them.

Respect

Repeatedly I have heard people say something to the effect, "If I'm going to show respect toward someone, it's got to be earned." This reveals an insensitive, demanding mind-set. It assumes that others must meet a proper standard to be treated decently.

Respect can be defined as demonstrating a regard for others, and recognizing their inherent God-given value. As an illustration of respectful behavior, we need look no further than the New Testament record of Jesus' interactions with others. One thing is certain: He had no requirement that His respect should be earned. Whether he was faced with the gravely ill, prostitutes, swindlers, children, wealthy citizens, or just plain ordinary folks, His initiative was consistent. He had no trouble being kind and uplifting whether the people in His presence had "earned" good treatment or not. Godly respect is not contingent upon the recipient meeting the correct criteria. Rather, it is a gift that is offered because the giver has chosen to do so.

When people divorce, a primary quality often lacking in their interpersonal exchanges is respect. I have heard numerous stories from divorcees who have been shunned or treated disrespectfully by those who either disapproved or misunderstood the reason for the divorce. Granted, some people initiate divorce for flimsy reasons, and this can cause Christian friends and family to feel perplexed or even disgusted as they observe the ill effects of watered-down family values. It is good to openly uphold the dignity of the marriage commitment, making known a preference for family cohesiveness and the self-restraint or sacrifice that goes along with it. That said, when we encounter individuals who are on the down side of a marital break-up, there is no excuse for Christians (or anyone else) to treat these individuals with disdain or disregard. You can give respect, as illustrated by Christ, even though you differ in beliefs or priorities. Sadly, I have heard Christian divorcees claim that they stopped going to church in favor of secular places. They have found non-Christians more willing to be respectful because their convictions are not so strong as to cause them to be disrespectful. What irony!

The Friday evening get-together with Kyle, Suzie, and Ron was the first of several such gatherings in the months that followed. "You know, it's a shame how friends can go long periods of time without contacting each other," Suzie remarked to Kyle, "and I don't want that to be repeated. Right now, more than ever, you need to be reminded that you're valued and loved."

"You're not just taking me on as a charity case, are you?" Kyle was kidding as he said it, but deep down he was probably fishing for some reassurance that his friends really cared.

"Well, maybe we are," she replied with a twinkle in her eye. Then getting serious she explained, "I know that some people don't understand why a divorce has to happen. In their confusion they can withdraw or maybe voice opposition that sounds judgmental. That's all the more motivation for Ron and me to let you know that you're still OK as far as we're concerned! We're going to make sure you don't forget that."

After the first visit to their home, Kyle returned to his apartment feeling tremendously relieved and blessed. In his own private musings, he reminded himself that God was not in the business of withdrawing His love whenever one of His own encountered difficult experiences like his. But this truth took on a whole new depth when friends such as Suzie and Ron stepped up to affirm that message. It was one thing for Kyle to know truth about God's love for him on an intellectual level, but the truth reached into his heart when Suzie and Ron embodied that love in the respect they gave so freely.

One woman, Kathy, explained her tension to me quite clearly when she said: "I'm often around other moms who seem to have no clue about how they are supposed to treat me as a divorced mother. They chat easily with each other, but when I'm in the mix, it's like their whole tone changes. For whatever reason, they can't relate to my situation of hustling home from work, picking up my daughter at her grandmother's house, then rushing her to her activities. Their lives are not so burdened by having to deal with an ex-husband or living well below the financial standards they had been accustomed to for years. All I'm wanting is to feel included and somewhat normal, not looked on as an outsider. You have no idea how healing that would be!"

Loving Curiosity

There are two extremes that can bother divorcees greatly. The first is the extreme of feeling as if they are required to offer an airtight explanation for their divorce. They soon learn that there are intrusive people waiting to hear the scoop about the marriage break-up so they can then determine whose fault it was. Knowing whose fault it was allows them to determine if they can continue the relationship, or if they should avoid the person all together.

The other extreme comes when others refuse to even acknowledge that the divorce has happened. Some people feel uncomfortable discussing anything personal. By refusing to talk about the divorce, these people send a negative message that gives divorcees the impression they have no desire to become involved with anything that might be distasteful or painful.

Kathy explained to me how she encountered both extremes. "There's a woman at my church who just *has* to have her nose in everyone else's business. She is known as a busybody and she loves juicy gossip. One Wednesday night, I was at the church to pick up my daughter from her choir rehearsal and this lady cornered me. She was syrupy sweet as she talked, and she started asking me extremely personal questions. She wanted to know if there had been another woman, if we'd had a history of major arguing, what our sex life had been like, and if I was financially destitute. I was amazed! It's like she was an investigative reporter who absolutely had to get to the bottom of the story."

"How did you handle this?" I asked.

"Well, I didn't trust her because she'd never really been very interested in me before my divorce. I just told her that I'd been through a rough time, and I wasn't ready to go into any great details." Then Kathy added, "The truth is, I have actually felt isolated in some instances and I wouldn't mind sharing my needs with friends. There are two women I can tell anything to, and that helps; but I would welcome some concern from my casual acquaintances, too. It's a great comfort when acquaintances just show an interest in my well-being. I'd be open with them if I sensed that their intentions were honorable."

Then shifting gears, she said: "I've been around several women who have known me for a couple of years or more, and in the past we've talked casually about our kids and family lives. I know they're aware of my current struggles and changes, but they won't ask me how I'm doing or mention anything at all about my divorce. There is a terribly superficial feeling that comes over our conversations because I'm very aware that they're avoiding the subject like a plague. That's just as uncomfortable as the intrusive communication."

By contrast, Kyle was affirmed in the way his friends, Suzie and Ron, responded to his struggles. On his first visit in their home, they told him: "We'd like to know about your divorce if you're comfortable with that. Most of all, we just want to know where you hurt or what your needs are so we can pray for you more specifically." Kyle was relieved that they would care enough to show such a level of concern. Another important factor was present that evening: he sensed no morbid curiosity from his two friends. Most of all, he knew he could trust them to be confidential as he discussed his pain with them.

People who have lived in a couples' world experience a tremendous jolt to their emotional system in the aftermath of divorce. They might feel as though they no longer fit in the same circles as before. As a result, loneliness can be a major emotional struggle, as can embarrassment or insecurity. More than ever, divorcees have a yearning to feel connected with individuals who truly care about their needs. The wounded divorcee is not likely to approach friends saying, "Well, I'm sure you want to know how I feel about my divorce, so let me give you the story." Uncertain about how some people will respond to their situation, they are more likely to wait for a friend to express a genuine interest in their needs. Divorcees *want* to be freed from their feelings of isolation. They usually welcome a trustworthy person who gently probes with an attitude of concern and love, and who draws them out of their isolation.

It is good to communicate an interest in the personal dimension of a divorcee's life. Though the subject of divorce or rejection can be an awkward one, it is a part of life that cannot be ignored. People like Kyle or Kathy feel a tremendous relief when others step forward with displays of interest and a desire to know. Certainly there are broad statements that can be made ("How are you adjusting to your new lifestyle routine?"). But there are moments when a more pointed statement can be appropriate too: "I can imagine that you've received varying reactions from family and friends. How have you been affected as the news of your divorce goes public?"

Years ago I learned that a long time acquaintance had been diagnosed with cancer. My first reaction was to pick up the phone and call to check on him. As soon as we made contact, I said, "Ted, I'm so concerned because I just heard you've been diagnosed with cancer. Tell me about your situation." His response was interesting. Before talking about his illness, he confided, "Do you realize how many people have talked with me *without* using the word 'cancer'? Thanks for calling it what it is." He then proceeded to tell me about his situation, and we had a very heartwarming exchange.

As I reflect on the conversation with my friend, it strikes me that it is far too common for people to dance endlessly around uncomfortable subjects. The dance goes on even when the person with the problem needs to hear that someone cares. Most hurting people welcome questions that reflect a loving spirit. If they are not ready to talk about it, they can let you know; but in most cases they are relieved once the subject is out in the open. Gentle and sensitive probing for the sake of gaining understanding is a means of keeping communication open. It reduces the isolation that too easily accompanies a marital split.

Empathy

Perhaps Christ's most powerful characteristic was His willingness to tune into people, as if He took their feelings and needs and made them His very own. Most people, for instance, would scorn lepers as too diseased to be loved; Jesus would look kindly into their eyes, touch them, and befriend them. Empathy was the quality that caused Him to ponder what it might be like to have a once-normal body riddled with numbness and infection. He would consider how hungry they were to feel understood, how badly they wanted once more to belong socially, and how insulted they felt when others shouted rejecting words.

Empathy can be defined as the ability to perceive another person's feelings and perceptions from that person's frame of reference. Reflecting further on the empathy of Christ, we are reminded that, being a part of the triune nature of God since before time, Christ was quite "other" in His relationship to depraved humanity. Stepping aside from His heavenly comfort, His entrance into humanity was the ultimate display of empathy. As a human, He would now experience unheavenly circumstances—being bitten by mosquitoes, having an upset stomach, feeling shunned by condescending know-it-alls, feeling weary from people pressing for their own selfish cravings. He realized that by taking the experiences of humanity upon Himself, Christ would then be positioned to communicate, with the highest credibility, His plan to redeem hurting people, showing them the way to God's better alternatives.

Just as empathy was an integral part of Jesus' style of positively influencing others, His followers today can use empathy to convey to others a message of love and respect. Empathy is especially necessary in times of pain, distress, or rejection. It is in times of trouble that people naturally wonder, "Do I matter? Does anyone really care? Could anyone possibly understand the emptiness that I feel?" When Christians display empathy, they are displaying a part of Jesus' character, making it easier for emotionally challenged people to grasp the reality that God is truly available and interested.

Once a divorce has gone public, many divorcees complain: "People have been so busy rendering opinions about what they think I should've done that they can't or won't take the time just to know me. I need someone to put an arm around me and acknowledge that I'm feeling hurt, angry, or bewildered." They have concluded that it is easier for many to give lots of unsolicited advice but little empathy. The result is that they may be driven away from God when they need Him most. They have learned the hard way that unsolicited advice has the same effect as criticism.

Kathy told me that she was unprepared for the onslaught of advice once news got out that she was getting divorced. She explained: "Too many people were ready to tell me what I should have done. I couldn't begin to count the times I've heard the phrase 'If I were you I would . . .' It's not that I didn't appreciate the concern that usually accompanied those remarks, but my main need often was *not* what I should do next. I needed someone to step forward just to acknowledge that it was OK to cry, to fume, or to feel dazed."

Kyle, on the other hand, explained that his renewed relationship with Suzie and Ron was a major ingredient in his healing. "Once I was talking to Ron about the awkwardness of getting used to sharing my family time with my two daughters. On their breaks from college, they had to float between my place and Vickie's, and that was difficult for all of us. When I told Ron about this, he quietly responded how parenting doesn't end when your kids go away to college. Even though the daily job of parenting has wound down, they still need guidance. He acknowledged that my frustration must lie in the fact that my role as a conscientious dad had been changed because of the divorce. He connected with how I yearn for them to be successful Christian women." Kyle's eyes lit up as he summarized: "That's all I needed to hear at the moment. It was refreshing to know that my friend understood what was in my mind and heart. I didn't need advice; I just needed to know that someone truly knew my heart."

That's empathy!

In empathizing, you demonstrate a willingness to set aside your current agenda in order to ponder the perspectives, needs, or feelings of another. You may not even agree fully with the other person's perspective, but agreement is not a required ingredient in empathy. Most people who have difficulty showing understanding toward another person are so concerned with being correct that they underestimate the power of a caring spirit. They fear that if they are too loving or accepting others might interpret them as soft regarding truth, which they deem to be the ultimate good. Although truth *is* an essential ingredient for balanced living, the personal dimension is even more essential. Love is most clearly communicated when people demonstrate an accepting and understanding spirit, *especially* amid pain, tension, and confusion.

Identification with Human Frailty (Me Too)

Kyle expressed a common discomfort experienced by many who have divorced: "Every person I know has had some sort of personal failure and disappointment. In fact, most people experience *many* personal hurts through the years. When your failure comes in the form of a divorce, though, you're not able to cover it up like you can cover other problems. I've known people who've had broken relations with friends or extended family members, but the general world has not known about it because at least they can go on living with some semblance of normalcy. But when you divorce, you feel like you've been placed naked on a stage with a big spotlight on you and everyone is invited to view exactly how flawed and imperfect you really are. It's like you have an extra amount of frailty on display as compared to everyone else."

Divorcees can experience feelings of unwanted uniqueness once their lifestyle becomes separate and distinct from those of their married counterparts. No longer able to hide the existence of a painful relationship, they often conclude that they do not fit in with their old surroundings because their failings are deemed more severe. As a result, these people need not just empathy but someone to step forward to say, "I've got flaws, just as you do." It helps for divorcees to know that life's playing field is level.

Kathy told me once, "My greatest frustration comes from the fact that I've been shunned by people who haven't been divorced but who have enough of their own character defects that they shouldn't be throwing stones." She gave an example of a woman whose daughter socialized with her child but who backed away once news of Kathy's divorce went public. "This woman has had all sorts of strains with members of her extended family, so she should know how painful it is to have gaping holes in key relationships. Instead, she seems afraid to identify too closely with me because she doesn't want to have to admit her own vulnerability to relationship breakdowns."

A major breakthrough came for Kathy when another mom in her circle of school acquaintances began sharing with her on a vulnerable level. "I've never been through a divorce," explained the friend, "but a couple of years ago I experienced major depression that was severe enough to put me in the hospital for a couple of weeks. My family and friends didn't know what to say to me or how to respond to my needs, and that was probably as hard on me as the depression itself. I had a lot of questions about my worth, and I had to get quite a bit of counseling to work through some erroneous thinking patterns. One thing I've learned because of my depression is that we all have feet of clay. I know that even though your circumstances are different, you must be experiencing your share of emotional ups and downs, so just know that I'll be there for you. I know what it's like to wonder if you're the only one who feels as you do."

The apostle Paul reminded his readers, "There is none righteous, not even one" (Romans 3:10). Yet when people like Kathy or Kyle have their unrighteousness exposed, they find that many pretend to be righteous, covering up their own humanness. What a relief it is when someone is bold enough to step forward, acknowledging that she too knows what it is like to go through unwanted struggle.

By identifying with another person's humanness, you are in essence communicating a belief in equality. You are registering the notion that no one can claim to be superior; nor should anyone be made to feel inferior in the presence of frailty. Failures, then, need not be construed as proof of lower value; rather, they can remind us of the wonderful truth that God deems us valuable despite of our shortcomings.

Encouragement

Divorcees need encouragement, a sense of hope and optimism regarding the future. Once they reach the point of divorce, they have already experienced large amounts of discouragement through coming to terms with the loss of a dream. As they start a new life, some may actually feel relief, while others feel apprehensive. Either way, they still face an unknown future and welcome any signals telling them that there is reason to believe they will be able to pursue realistic dreams once again.

Kyle explained this to his friends Ron and Suzie: "I've never been a fifty-something single guy before. This is all new territory for me. I've been in plenty of situations in the past, both in business and family, where I've had to be decisive, but nothing I've experienced could prepare me to know how to handle the aftermath of divorce. I've had confidence in my past coping skills, so I assume that I'll be able to draw on my abilities again in this situation. But I'll tell you—it sure helps having friends on the sidelines reminding me that they're pulling for me every step of the way. You never know how meaningful encouragement is until you've come in contact with a great unknown."

In the early 1970s, as a college student, I had an experience that starkly illustrated the difference between encouragement and discouragement. One Friday evening, I was working at the front desk of a motel and received a phone call from one of our guests. A frightened male voice said, "I've taken an overdose of pills and I'm afraid I might die; you've got to help me." Immediately I summoned an ambulance. Then I had the presence of mind to take salt with me to the man's room. I had the man drink salt water, which induced vomiting. After cleaning him up, we went outside to sit on the porch for some fresh air. As we awaited medical treatment, he conveyed how he was under work-related stress while simultaneously struggling with his marriage. Clearly embarrassed, the man apologized profusely for causing such a commotion, but I put my arm around him and assured him that I was there to help.

In just a few moments, a gruff, overweight law officer found me sitting with this man with his head tucked between his knees. If the circumstances had been less serious, it would have seemed funny that this fellow was the perfect stereotype of the waddling, pot-bellied deputy that seems to appear in movies depicting law enforcement corruption in the Deep South. With a deep, blustery voice he bellowed, "Why in the hell would you do something stupid like this, son? What in God's name is wrong with you anyway?" I wanted to kick the old coot, but better judgment prevailed as I just quietly put my arm on his shoulders and said, "Don't worry; we'll get you through this." The man looked at me with tears in his eyes and said quietly, "I really need to hear that."

In the years since, I've learned that people who will not encourage are fearful. They are afraid that soft emotions or gentle words of comfort reflect a fundamental character flaw, when instead they reflect the very kindness of God. Those who encourage feel privileged to be a bright spot in the presence of one who is vulnerable and feels defeated. They realize that we all yearn to be affirmed as significant despite our heartaches and setbacks. Encouragers realize a life-changing power comes upon people when they hear the words "I believe in you."

When you encourage, you may be temporarily required to set aside your opinions of right and wrong, realizing that the one in need wants words of support more than advice. Your encouragement can be your way of conveying, "Though we differ in our circumstances, we are equal in the need to be uplifted. This is what you deserve, and this is what you'll receive from me."

All of the traits listed in this chapter (respect, loving curiosity, empathy, identification with humanness, encouragement) are part of the process of bearing burdens with one another. Galatians 6:2 tells us that when we bear burdens we "fulfill the law of Christ." Since Christ was not a fussy person who insisted upon impeccable performance, what then is His law? Love. Though divorce may present a set of problems you cannot fully comprehend, your commitment to Christ can still propel you to be His loving representative.

Chapter Ten

What About Grace Abusers?

As Carl sat in his pastor's office telling him for the first time the news about his pending divorce, he looked shell-shocked, like someone who had just been through a major trauma. "We've been married seventeen years," he explained, "and I've felt for the last ten years that we were on shaky ground, but now that the divorce is happening, I'm at a loss. I don't know what I'm supposed to say or do. I don't have a clue about how this will affect our fourteen-year-old son. I'm just numb. At work, we're going through a light period, which is good because if we had some stringent projects going, I'd be very ineffective."

Michael, the pastor, was sympathetic as he listened. He had been aware for a couple of years that this marriage was in jeopardy, so the news of its demise certainly was no shock. Michael assured Carl that he wanted him to continue participating in the church's programs as he had in the past, adding, "Now more than ever you need to know your church is here for you. We love you and we want you to remain strong in your love for God."

A few weeks later, one of the pastor's close friends told him: "My wife and I went to a restaurant on a week night and in the bar area we saw Carl with a group that was doing some major partying. He never saw us, so we didn't speak. Let's just say it was obvious that he was intoxicated and on very friendly terms with one of the women there." In the weeks that followed, Michael heard similar reports from other people that Carl had dropped most of his ties with Christian friends and was playing the field with various women.

With his increasing party behavior, Carl's commitment to church activities or time with Christian friends shrank drastically. When his Christian friends sought him out to be supportive, he would speak to them in "Christian lingo" about searching for the Lord's will in this new phase of life; but associating with his new party friends, he rarely mentioned his church, much less his relationship with Christ. In a period of a few months, Carl went from being a man heavily involved in his church and committed to a daily walk with the Lord to being a man with loose morals. It seemed he was turning his back on the way of life he had once held dear.

Perhaps an analogy can explain what is happening in Carl's mind. Consider what life is like for a dog that lives inside a fenced backyard. The yard may be beautifully landscaped, and the dog may even be fed T-bone steaks every day. However, as the dog sees the fence hemming it in day after day, one thought dominates its mind: "Get me out of here!" When the gate swings open, the dog runs and invariably is indiscriminate regarding where it goes or what it does.

Sometimes divorcing people resemble the dog running outside the fence. For years, perhaps, they have felt imprisoned by a relationship that was unrewarding. They have tried to keep up a good front by doing the right things, but once they decide to end the marriage, they think, "Look out, freedom, here I come!" Weary from a past that has been most burdensome, they are thrilled to know that they can make choices without having to answer to a restrictive spouse. Only when they "run" do they truly realize that their propriety during their marriage was more a function of duty than choice. Embracing their newfound freedom (which is a cornerstone of grace), these people can rationalize to themselves that they need fewer restraints—and in some instances, that thinking can be risky.

A couple of men from a former Bible study group of Carl's met with him one morning over breakfast. Their intent was to discuss the rumors floating around about his new way of life and to encourage him to stay connected to his Christian friends who wanted to love him through his transition. These men truly cared for Carl and had a solid history of being gracious with him. As the conversation unfolded, Carl became defensive and said to his friends, "I don't need the legalistic crowd to come down on me so they can monitor my every move. If your goal is to reform me and fit me into your rigid mold, I'll have nothing more to do with you!" The two friends were dumbfounded by his outburst.

People like Carl frequently have a history of letting their Christian values be externally driven as opposed to internally driven. Though they may have a history of living according to right values, once the marriage ends they feel exposed and vulnerable. At this point they can either move to reaffirm their love and gratitude for the goodness of God's principles and fellowship with God's people, or they can decide to see what's on the other side and experiment with ungodly behavior. Usually in selecting the latter option they appeal to grace, stating, "I need to be accepted for what I am as opposed to living in a crummy mold like I did in my marriage."

There is often an element of truth in the sentiments of people like Carl. It *is* good to claim acceptance from God during a failure. It *is* good to realize that a successful life is not defined by living inside a perfect mold. It *is* good to entertain choices about where to go in future lifestyle decisions. The error in their thinking, however, is to fall upon grace in order to excuse choices that are inconsistent with godliness. They are thus abusing grace—a problem that needs to be monitored carefully in the aftermath of divorce. Most divorcees are faced with decisions that are no longer controlled by the veto of a spouse who thinks contrary to them, and if previously their good behavior was driven more by external than internal motivations then they can become vulnerable to rationalizing poor choices.

Misusing God's Grace

Let's take a look at some of the most common factors that show a person to be taking advantage of God's grace in the aftermath of divorce.

Experimentation with Questionable Values

Haley was a stepmom who had been married for just five months to Jeff. They met through mutual friends and enjoyed a highly satisfying love. Jeff shared joint custody of his six-year-old son, Cody, who lived with his mom, Callie. Jeff and Haley sought counseling, not because they were having marital problems but because they were wondering how best to deal with his ex-wife, Callie.

To say that Callie was a free spirit would be a great understatement. In her early thirties, she was beautiful and financially secure. She had made many new friends in the three years since her divorce. Though the courts decreed that she would keep Cody during the week and every other weekend, she frequently called Haley to keep Cody overnight, sometimes as often as three or four times a week. Even on her designated weekends, Callie would tell her ex-husband, "Why don't you just let Cody stay with you this weekend? He's been asking about you a lot." What she meant was, "I have social plans, and he'll be in the way."

Callie had a history of being closely associated with Christians. In her teens and college years, she belonged to organizations that promoted Christian character and taught the principles of the Bible well. In fact, she and Jeff met during a Bible study. Once they married, however, Callie became increasingly loose in her decision making. She allowed alcohol a central role in her social life, and she openly endorsed the party scene. She joined a workout club with a girlfriend from work, and there she encountered men who would flirt with her and make flattering remarks about her beauty, something that stroked her ego greatly. Weekends were increasingly filled with escapades with her drinking buddies, even after their son was born. This meant, then, that it was easier to put church plans for Sunday on the back burner because she was spending more Saturday nights out late with her new friends. By the time she and Jeff divorced, she was hardly associating with any Christians at all and did little to teach young Cody about the Lord.

If asked about her Christianity, Callie would say: "I'm just as much of a Christian as anyone else, but I'm not tied down with guilt and restrictions like I used to be." Indeed, Callie's earlier understanding of Christianity focused more on its dos and don'ts than on the beauty of God's grace. Now, in her pursuit of a less constrictive way of live, the pendulum swung too far in the other direction.

Does this sound familiar? Prior to divorce, it is common for individuals to experience a build-up of anger, with its residual resentment and frustration. Usually these people have felt thwarted in releasing their emotions, so when the shackles of an unhappy marriage are discarded it is easy to allow that emotion to run full throttle. Pent-up anger is the fuel that feeds rebellious behavior, and though the newly divorced person may not acknowledge the ongoing role of that anger it can remain a major factor in establishing new priorities.

Instead of admitting that there is a problem with anger or rebelliousness, many of these people deny it. "I'm not at all angry," the reasoning may go, "I just have realized that Christianity is not a list of right and wrong, but it's a gift that frees us from having to adhere to strict standards before we can be accepted. I really like God's grace!"

Even though grace is indeed a wonderful gift that does not require us to live perfectly before receiving God's abundant love, it does not also give us license to knowingly embrace behavior that is inconsistent with godliness.

A Spirit of Entitlement

As people appeal to grace while behaving rebelliously, it is common for the appeal to be accompanied by a spirit of entitlement. Having gone outside the limits of their formerly conservative behavior, they now expect people to simply go along with their aberrant choices. They do not intend to mend their ways. Grace abusers, then, can become demanding, even pushy, as they project an attitude that implies, "You owe it to me to offer unconditional acceptance." In an effort to bolster their behavior, they salve their conscience by wrongly interpreting the strong convictions and concerns of others as judgmental.

The two friends who visited Carl over breakfast to discuss their concerns about his changing lifestyle were not the only ones who felt uneasy about his new priorities. Other friends and relatives also talked with him about the downward spiral he was in, but none succeeded in penetrating the shell around his heart. Admittedly, some spoke to him with a condescending spirit, but many truly had good intentions. Rather than being judgmental, his Christian friends feared that Carl would forsake his lifestyle of purity for one of self-indulgence and continue the downhill spiral.

Despite the clean motives of these concerned people, Carl's consistent response was, "Who do these people think they are, telling me how to run my life? I can recall plenty of incidents in the past when I was there for them in their down times. They owe it to me to support me through my tough situation."

Was Carl on target with this sentiment? Certainly it was reasonable for him to want support from people he had known for years. After all, the Bible *does* teach us to bear one another's burdens. In this case, rather than merely looking to his friends for support Carl was really asking them to drop their convictions of right and wrong in order to overlook his obviously poor choices.

Carl, like many in his position, was generalizing, causing him to misinterpret his loved ones' concerns. Because there was a high probability that *someone* in the Christian world would harshly judge him, he wrongly assumed that *everyone* who had differing opinions would be judgmental. In reality, even if Carl had admitted that he was disillusioned with Christianity and was taking a break in order to explore other alternatives, some of Carl's friends would have been patient enough to say, "I'm still here for you through it all."

For anyone feeling the need to fall upon God's grace, a demanding spirit is counterproductive. Sincere acknowledgment of the need for grace is accompanied not by a prideful spirit but by humility. True humility never prompts one to shake a fist and shout, "You owe me!" Rather, it energizes a healing person to quietly appreciate others' kindness and concern.

Refusal to Admit Faults

In talking with people in the aftermath of divorce, I see one major characteristic indicating whether they are likely to experience growth and healing. It is the willingness to admit faults. No divorcee can look upon all the problems of the marriage and claim, "I was the epitome of composure and stability through all our marital ups and downs." The problems leading to divorce inevitably include tension, anger, miscommunication, bitterness, and insecurity. The divorcees who can say "I am willing to identify some definite areas for self-improvement" are the ones who have the best chance for growth. They know that it is during times of crisis and pain that God's healing touch can be most creative and real.

Divorcees attempting to minimize their negatives usually accompany the effort with a need to blame the former partner for personal failures. Growth, then, is less likely. Even though divorce may be precipitated by only one errant marriage partner, and even in an incident where a divorcee was more the victim than the victimizer, there is still room for the other to admit failings. However, grace abusers assume that if they admit faults others will judge them, so the way to prevent that possibility is to cover up.

If I see a divorcee trying too hard to put on a correct front, I advise: "Like it or not, you will be scrutinized when you go through a divorce. In their curiosity, people will want to know what went wrong. Rather than just asking for blanket approval for all you've ever done, it is actually a sign of maturity when you can admit where you stumbled." (By the way, I also tell divorcees that some folks are just plain nosy and can be too forward in their need to know. There are times when it is OK to politely let them know that your flaws are none of their concern. Discretion regarding self-disclosure is always reasonable.)

Those who will not admit humanness are typically so consumed with their "right" to receive grace that they forget to see it for what it is: an unexpected gift.

A Refusal to Be Accountable

When Christian brothers or sisters reach the end of a failed marriage, it is good for fellow believers to come to their side and help them get back on their feet. For instance, many Christians going through divorce hope that they can still participate fully in church life, but it may take some time for others to reestablish full confidence in their leadership capabilities. Even the divorcees who are comparatively "innocent" find it advisable to curtail some church responsibilities in order to allow the healing process to run its course.

Mature divorcees do not just acknowledge their accountability; they welcome the prospect. They know that they need the objective observation of others who might eventually help them find ways to be more relationally and spiritually whole. For instance, Yvonne told me that as she went through her divorce she decided it would be best to step away for a while from responsibilities in teaching youths at her church. A couple of months after her new single life began, a close friend told her, "You've been so much more relaxed and peaceful recently. Several months ago, I could tell that you were struggling with hidden frustrations, but now your demeanor has become much calmer." Yvonne later told me that she had no idea she displayed her frustrations so clearly; she thought she was doing a successful job hiding them. "I really need some time just to make sure I am getting my house in order, and right now I'm very open to the feedback my friends give me about my past because I'd definitely like to learn from their perspectives."

Grace abusers have great difficulty in assuming an attitude like Yvonne's. Too many of these people portray a mind-set that implies, "I don't need anyone scrutinizing my life, thank you, and I shouldn't be expected to take a break from my responsibilities just because of my divorce." False pride begins to dominate their personalities as they display a smug spirit, or as they assume that there is little they need to learn from their experience. In contrast, people like Yvonne recognize that the greatest personal growth tends to occur during crisis, so they willingly pull back from extra demands in order to open their minds to new directions. Grace abusers, however, demand that their crises be set aside as quickly as possible. They should not be expected to slow down and enter a new learning process.

Responding to Grace Abuse

I always try not to respond to divorcees with harshness or rejection. People going through a painful time in their life need fellow believers who will accept them in the Lord and be an encouraging presence as they move forward in the many adjustments to come. This does not mean, however, that there are never times to talk straight with divorcees who flirt with personal disaster or who refuse to take advantage of growth opportunities. The challenge for the church and Christian friends is to respond as appropriately as possible so God's love can still be experienced, and if possible Christian fellowship can be enhanced, not lost.

Let's examine how a spirit of grace can still be extended as people in recovery from divorce move in the wrong direction.

Realize That the Person Is Hurting

What do you think about the way Carl was handling his lifestyle as he tried on new behaviors as a single man? If you are like me, you probably would agree that it was not at all good for him to adopt the "wine, women, and song" routine. Apparently, Carl had felt stifled by the values of his Christian life and was ready to expand into what he perceived as a new world of adventure—ignoring the reality that a whole new set of problems awaited him.

Did Carl need reprimanding? guidance? confrontation? Let's put it this way: if he were a close friend or relative of mine, I would have a hard time watching his life disintegrate without saying *something* to him. So, yes, it would be appropriate to speak openly and honestly about the issues he is facing.

But (you knew there would be a "but") before talking with someone like Carl about errant behavior, it is of the utmost importance that you truly understand his heart, even if you do not agree with his choices. A person like Carl who is acting out is hurting. Pain is factoring into his decisions. So before discussing his poor choices and decisions, it is first helpful to connect on the inner level where his pain exists.

I once spoke with a recent divorcee who began an extramarital affair with a married man shortly after her divorce was final. She was emotionally torn and confused about the direction of her life; a friend suggested she see me for counseling. Reluctantly, she came to my office and told me her story. In the first session, I gathered as much information as I could about her life, her family history, her unmet needs, and her confusion about the failure of her marriage. In the second session, we talked about how a hidden anger was fueling her life. It propelled her to take on a protective attitude: "I've got to take care of my needs as best as I can because no one else will." The affair was obviously an issue that needed to be addressed and understood, but I recognized that this woman had a much more pressing need to delve into the emotional pain driving her to pursue an illicit relationship.

After her second visit with me, this woman paused as she exited my office and said, "I need to tell you something. Before I came to counseling, I was worried that you'd disapprove of me once you heard my story." I explained to her that although I do indeed have beliefs about right and wrong, I felt we would meet our therapeutic goals more readily if we first focused on the pain that lay beneath her current choices. "We can eventually talk more frankly about the decisions that are best for you, but first I need to understand your heart."

Perhaps you are familiar with the saying, "People don't care how much you know until they know how much you care." This thought is especially applicable when people are discussing lifestyle adjustments that have occurred in the aftermath of divorce. Too often, well-intended helpers rush in with advice and suggestions for the straying person before truly establishing a caring spirit. (Untimely advice is virtually always perceived as rejection.) Perhaps a statement or two will be made in an attempt to quickly establish concern, and *then* the advice flows. In most cases, the hurting person needs more than a statement or two of concern. Advice has its place, though only after personal matters are fully known. Once a full pattern of care is established, it is amazing how strong your long-term influence can be.

To be helpful, you probably need to approach errant people with *patience* first, and then once that is established it is best to apply *patience*, followed directly with a solid dose of *patience*. In due time, it may be necessary to be direct about issues of morality or about the values that underlie various pursuits. But before you are fully heard, you may need to let out some rope as you demonstrate a willingness to accept others as they are. In the best-case scenario, your understanding of their hurting spirit is the very tool that will eventually cause a straying person to resume more balanced priorities. Kindness attracts.

Speak Open-Endedly About the Troublesome Issues

Once your patience and acceptance are well established (it may take ten minutes or ten weeks or ten months), you may find it appropriate to confront the problems you see in the person who is abusing grace. "Speaking truth in love" (as it says in Ephesians 4:15), you are certainly justified to probe errant matters. For instance, it was reasonable for Carl's friends to talk with him about the fact that his new party life had taken priority over his commitment to Christian friendships. The key to this step is to not try to pin down a commitment to change *now*.

To illustrate, let's suppose Carl's friends said, "We've heard about your sleeping around with other women and getting drunk. This has to stop right away, so when do you plan to repent?" How would Carl likely respond? In all probability, he would become defensive and leave feeling rejected and more isolated than ever from the Christian community. Every now and then, the blunt or frontal approach to confrontation may be necessary, but in most instances, there is a better way.

As an alternative, Carl's friends might say something like, "In the past, we used to get some time in to play a round of golf. I know your schedule has changed now, but I don't want to lose touch with you. I know you've been through some tough changes and I'd like an update on how you are doing." The probabilities of his positive receptiveness would increase greatly. He would be more likely to think, "Wow! You miss my company! I'm glad to know you care." Stretching out this illustration, let's suppose the friends do play golf with Carl a few days later, and one remarks, "I'm aware you've made new friends lately and have pursued activities separate from some of your old church buddies. Help me understand: What's different in your thinking these days?"

Now a discussion can develop. A shift in priorities can be aired. Changes in philosophy and beliefs can be explored. The errant person is probably already aware of your differing beliefs and priorities, and he already knows where you would like to see him make adjustments. Also, it is usually not necessary for you to give a persuasive speech in the hope that you will shed new light on that person's problems. This does not mean that you should never speak about your differing opinions, because sometimes it is fully appropriate to let your perspective be heard. However, if the erring person is going to be able to absorb what you have to say, it will happen best out of a caring dialogue, not a harsh monologue. Speak honestly about your issues, but make plenty of room for the possibility that the other person may not change immediately. Allow the other person time to digest your discussions. Don't be so forceful right away that your controlling demeanor overshadows your message of concern. Don't abuse grace by trying to change a grace abuser.

As an example, a man told me about the delicate way his friend Jason helped him during a downward spiral after a second divorce: "A lot of people had given up on me because I was now seen as a two-time loser. I quit going to church because, frankly, I didn't feel that I'd measure up to the values everyone there held. I started going to happy hours after work with non-Christians and soon you could hardly tell any difference between them and me in the way we lived and talked.

"When Jason called me to say he wanted to talk with me, I knew exactly where he wanted to go. He wanted me to quit this new non-Christian way of life. I was reluctant at first to make time for him because the last thing I needed was a well-intended morality lecture. But when we got together, I was pleasantly surprised that he didn't seem overeager to force me back into the Christian mold. I came from a strong Christian family, and I had already felt ostracized by my parents and my brother. But Jason simply told me he felt he needed to spend more time with me.

"We'd see each other at least once a week, and we played tennis, went to sporting events, had lunch. Occasionally, I went with him to a men's prayer breakfast, and it reminded me how I missed the kind of friendship you can form at church. It took several months, but I finally returned to church and started getting my priorities back in line. I give a lot of credit to Jason because he was so understanding in the way he handled things with me. Whenever we'd be together, he freely talked about the Lord's goodness, but not once did he preach to me. He was exactly what I needed at a very low time in my life."

Jason was aware that others had been quite outspoken about this man's latest divorce, so he made a deliberate decision to accept him, flawed and confused as he was. When Jason brought up the subject of the failed marriage, it was never in a way that seemed harsh. He would ask "How's your daughter handling the transition?" or say "I'm guessing your life isn't following the script you once thought it would." To address his abandonment of former Christian priorities, Jason would say something like, "When a marriage collapses, it can cause you to question lots of things that once were central to your life."

Such comments were Jason's way of keeping the doorway of communication open, and he determined that he would be in no hurry to reform his friend. Over time, the two enjoyed many discussions regarding the friend's value system and his questions about the validity of Christian morals. Knowing that unsolicited advice has a way of sounding like criticism, Jason was careful to portray himself as confident in his own beliefs but not intrusive. He knew that his friend's struggles did not arise overnight, and they would not go away overnight. He also could recall a period of time in his own past when he was rebellious, remembering how he was ultimately influenced by loving Christians who lived out goodness as opposed to preaching to him about it.

For Christians confronting straying believers, a common mistake is pushing truth onto a person before the individual is ready to absorb it. Of course, it is necessary to stand up for godly convictions, but it is of utmost importance to remember that *the relationship is the message*.

Sometimes, Withdrawal May Be Necessary

If you have spent much time at all trying to help hurting people, you are aware that sometimes your message is not well received, no matter how patient or loving you are. Stories abound from the life of Christ that show how His accepting spirit prepared the hearts of people to hear His message of change. The interaction with the Samaritan woman at the well (recorded in John 4) and the woman caught in adultery (John 8) are good illustrations of people who received His message as a direct result of His patient approach. But even Jesus Christ's message was poorly received at times, as is illustrated by the rich young ruler and Judas Iscariot.

Cynicism and resentment can cause divorced people to refuse any input from Christian friends, no matter how kindly it is communicated. If such a reaction remains persistent, withdrawal from fellowship may be in order. This is not meant to be a punishment to the straying person, but it may be necessary as a means of indicating you are not enabling poor choices.

As an illustration, Ron was very active in his local church. Over the years, he taught Sunday School, served on numerous committees, and established himself as one of the more likeable men in the congregation. When word got out that Ron and his wife were divorcing, it wasn't long before rumors of another woman began emerging. Once the divorce was final, Ron moved in with his new girlfriend and declared to his family and friends that he had never been so happy in all his life. Pleas from his children and longtime friends fell on deaf ears as it became apparent to all that Ron had convinced himself that he was making a reasonable choice and that God was certainly kind enough to accept the fact that his new relationship, though not exactly managed according to the rules, was indeed a good one.

For months, Ron continued living with the woman without the benefit of marriage, and then eventually he began bringing her to church services as well as to his old Sunday School class. As soon as it was obvious that numerous people seemed uneasy with this arrangement, he complained to some of his friends, "I thought Christianity was all about forgiveness, but I sure don't see it in the faces of all these would-be judges."

Was Ron wrong to appeal to his need for his friends' forgiveness? Not really. It is good and necessary to forgive one another since none of us is ever above the need for it ourselves. Ron's error in reasoning, though, was in assuming that forgiveness requires the giver of it to simultaneously abandon convictions of right and wrong. His demanding spirit clouded his logic.

Establishing ethical or moral boundaries is not a matter of an unforgiving spirit. The church indeed should be known as a haven for sinners, but it is not required to take an anything-goes philosophy. Matthew 18:15–17 records the words of Jesus that apply to a case where truth is shunned: "And if your brother sins, go and reprove him in private; if he listens to you, you have won your brother. But if he does not listen to you, take one or two more with you so that by the mouth of two or three witnesses every fact may be confirmed. And if he refuses to listen to them, tell it to the church; and if he refuses to listen even to the church, let him be to you as a Gentile and a tax gatherer."

Of all people, Jesus was not one to be impatient and insensitive to the hurts of people who were straying. Yet even He realized that some people cling so stubbornly to wrong priorities that it can regrettably be necessary to remove a person from fellowship.

After it became clear that Ron was maintaining a cavalier attitude about his affair and live-in relationship, the senior minister at his church said to him: "As much as I love you, I'm not able to encourage you to participate in any influential roles as long as you won't let go of your new priorities. I want you to know the grace and forgiveness of God, but I personally don't want to be guilty of insinuating that it's OK to receive God's goodness and then turn your back on His plan for a fulfilling life. At some point, we have to draw the line and lovingly say that what you are doing is wrong."

He and Ron chatted for over an hour, but it became clear that Ron would have nothing to do with his church's stand. Consequently, he permanently broke ties with the people there.

It is sad indeed when someone like Ron does not receive the goodness of God's ways and stubbornly insists that it is both proper and necessary to continue wrong pursuits. But as Ron's minister explained, at some point it is necessary to establish a boundary.

As a general rule, it is usually good for a divorcing person to take a break from leadership roles in the church in order to allow healing to occur. There are times when this move may not be necessary, so let's not be dogmatic about it; nonetheless, most divorces entail a heavy emotional toll, so it is good to let divorcees be ministered to, as opposed to being the one others are leaning on. In time (and again it is not necessary to be dogmatic about how long) you will be able to see how the divorcee is responding to personal changes, and it may be perfectly reasonable to suggest that normal practices resume. But because there are always going to be some who respond to such a major transition poorly, it is reasonable to establish that the church is showing itself to be responsible by maintaining standards for its members who want to participate in full standing.

At this point, let's reiterate that not all divorcees should immediately be deemed sinners in need of thorough regeneration. Many married or single people in the church experience problems far worse than what the divorcee is experiencing. Often the difference is in the fact that the divorcee's personal problems just happen to be more public. With that said, it is reasonable to lovingly watch over those in crisis for the purpose of holding firmly to standards of godliness.

Honest Introspection

Those in a position of dealing with potential grace abusers do well to first search their own hearts to determine how they would like to be treated if the roles were reversed. Not one of us is immune from poor decision making, so even if we have not erred as another has, we can still recognize how fragile a person is when a major life shake-up occurs.

Jason, the man who patiently and gently shepherded his straying divorced friend back onto a path of morality, explained how he was able to project a genuine spirit of love to his friend. "When I was in college, I had problems with drugs and alcohol. Often I gave the impression that I was just a disaster waiting to happen. Actually, I wanted the more secure life offered in Christianity, but I wasn't sure yet what God would require of me, and frankly, listening to God was not a high priority. Fortunately, a mentor saw the good in me even as I continued to make stupid decisions, and he never left my side. I was so moved by his loyalty to me that I became increasingly willing to consider his philosophy of life. Now, whenever I encounter someone who seems to be questioning life's priorities, I recall those moments when I didn't have life completely figured out, and I cut them some slack, just like my mentor did for me."

As Jason saw his friend struggle, his introspective nature led him to determine that a caring spirit is far more influential than an abrupt attempt to set a wanderer back onto the right path. His honesty caused him to remember that he did not come to understand the balance between God's grace and justice after just one or two discussions. His steadiness in the face of his friend's unsteadiness serves as a powerful example that many will return to the message of God's goodness if it is displayed with unmistakable concern.

Chapter Eleven

Why Are People Judgmental?

Most judgmental people do not think of themselves as graceless or unloving. Most of them have a good track record of being nice to people, of offering assistance, of even going out of their way to extend care where there is a critical need. Rightly, they would point to such behavior and claim, "How can anyone not appreciate my commitment to goodness?" Indeed, it would be hard to argue that much of their life is incompatible with grace.

I find it interesting that many people embrace the need to extend grace in numerous circumstances *except* divorce. For some reason, we can accept an array of problems among church members yet hold to strict, even harsh standards regarding divorce. To underscore the inconsistency of this thinking, it would be interesting to conduct a survey of those in professional church positions as well as laity who serve on church committees and as deacons, elders, and teachers. We might ask: Have you ever told a lie or borne false witness? Have you ever dishonored your mother or father? Have you ever not kept the Sabbath holy? Have you had any problems with anger? Have you ever neglected your body through poor diet or excess weight? Has there ever been a time when you've lusted? Have you ever spoken God's name in a less-than-honoring way? Do you always forgive when it is appropriate, or has forgiveness ever proven elusive? Do you always speak truth in love, or has there ever been another motive in how you present truth? Have you ever stolen? Do you neglect the needy? Have you ever disciplined your children with harshness? Do you always show understanding to your wife or husband? Do you have a quiet and gentle spirit? Have you ever held onto bitterness?

Do you have any tensions with members of your extended family that have gone unresolved? Are you ever stubborn or quarrelsome?

I suspect if we went to any church and posed such questions to every church leader (professional or lay), we would encounter many red-faced individuals. It is a certainty that every church, regardless of denominational affiliation, is packed with people who have *something* in their personal history that forces them to appeal to the grace of God. No one is even remotely close to being able to claim righteousness on his or her own merits.

Why, then, do some people continue to cling to judgment, often applying it arbitrarily or inconsistently? What pushes such an attitude?

I had an interesting series of discussions with a man we'll refer to as Keith. For years, he pastored growing churches and developed a reputation as someone who taught the word of God with great enthusiasm and conviction. Possessing an engaging personality and a fine sense of humor, this man was widely respected as a delightful speaker.

As a minister, he was often asked to perform marriage ceremonies, and through the years he officiated at many weddings. He took special care to inject personal comments regarding the bride and groom each time he married a couple, and it was well known that Keith would create an upbeat atmosphere on such an occasion. He had one rule, though, that he followed strictly. He would not perform a wedding for anyone who had been divorced unless he was convinced they had divorced on biblical grounds. If the potential bride or groom's former spouse were an unreformed alcoholic, an abuser, or grossly neglectful, he would express sympathy regarding the difficulties that this must have presented, but he would always refer the couple to another minister to perform the wedding. He would not compromise his convictions.

A problem arose for Keith that truly conflicted him. His daughter, Monica, married once she finished college, and soon she discovered that her husband had embezzled money from his employer. The young man avoided criminal prosecution on the provision that he would repay the money, which he did. Within a year, he repeated the same criminal act with his next employer, but this time he did not get off quite so easily. He was prosecuted for the crime and sentenced to eight years in prison. The young couple lost thousands of dollars in legal fees, and the young wife learned that he had borrowed thousands of dollars from friends, apparently with no intention of paying it back.

As Monica talked with him about her ordeal with her husband, Keith learned that her husband had treated her quite poorly. He was a habitual liar and was rarely reliable in following through on any commitment. She had spent hours arguing and crying with him as she attempted to get him to make the changes necessary to get their marriage on the right track, but to no avail. In time, the pressure was so great that the marriage ended in divorce.

Several years later, Monica fell in love with a responsible man who was respected by all as having great integrity and Christian virtue. They decided to marry, so he and Monica did what any pastor's daughter would do: they asked her father to perform the wedding ceremony. Keith truly liked the new fiancé, and he knew he would be an excellent son-in-law. But there was obviously a problem: Monica had not divorced on biblical grounds and he had his standards to keep. He had personally led the first husband to the Lord and baptized him when he was a teen, so he could not declare that Monica was ever abandoned by a nonbeliever. Likewise, there was no adultery. So was Keith going to turn his back on his own daughter now that she had the opportunity to start a new life with a truly good man?

It was at this point that Keith reconsidered his beliefs about divorce and remarriage. He openly confessed: "When it was someone else's son, daughter, sister, or brother who had gone through divorce, I would sympathize with them about the pain they must have felt, but in my mind I'd state that *someone* has got to stand up for what was right. But now I was faced with the possibility of turning away my own child, someone I have loved so dearly that literally I would sacrifice my own life for her. How could I risk giving her the message that I couldn't bless her unless she had lived life according to my lofty standards?"

It was at this personal crossroad that Keith encountered God's grace in a whole new light. He realized that God's character bound him to teach perfect principles to his flock. Yet Keith began to grapple with the reality that every one of us—himself included—falls short of that perfect standard in some fashion. Some may fall short by making a wrong marriage selection, others by failing in parenting, and others by being imperfect in matters of morality. Seeing this, Keith also realized that God did not give grace discriminately, offering it to some sinners but withholding it from others depending on the actual nature of the sin. His love for his own daughter caused him to show flexibility in his love of divorcees, though it did not mean that he had to give up his convictions about the sanctity of marriage. Instead, it opened up a whole new capacity to minister to those in his church who had failed in marriage.

The Problem with Judgmentalism

In talking with people like Keith who are trying to emerge from the heavy burden of representing God correctly, I emphasize several principles.

Idealism Does Not Always Match Reality

In my imagination, I am capable of conjuring up all sorts of fantasies about the perfect relationship. For instance, I can picture a family life where my wife and I understand each other's every mood, where our conversations are consistently encouraging, where our kids have no heartaches, where the extended family harmonizes wonderfully on special occasions, where we have no financial setbacks. Give me a lazy Saturday afternoon by the pool to just sit and dream, and I can make all my problems go away in the intoxicating world of imagination.

When I snap back to reality, wouldn't you know, I find that such understanding, peace, harmony, and bliss are quite a bit more elusive. It's fun to fantasize perfection, but I'd better stay prepared for moments of misunderstanding, disharmony, conflict, disease, and unexpected setbacks. That's just the way life is in the real world.

No matter how seemingly nice or balanced, everyone needs to make plenty of preparation for the lack of perfection. We simply do not exist in an ideal world. Yet as clearly as we can see the reality of imperfection in many aspects of life, there are believers who refuse to make room for reality in their theology. They do rules with a vengeance, particularly regarding a subject like divorce. In their mind, accepting the reality of failed ideals is the same as condoning them.

Jeremiah 17:9 is one of the most unflattering verses in the Bible: "The heart is more deceitful than all else and is desperately sick; who can understand it?" There is no way to get around the truth that every human, without exception, is capable of disappointing God greatly. This core truth is set aside, though, as some cling staunchly to the ideal that surely, with lots of sound instruction, we can motivate people to shed their tendency to do wrong and steer them instead toward doing everything the way it's supposed to be done. Though it is noble, of course, to aim for God's lofty ideals, we can still minister and love each other *when* (not *if*) those ideals are not met.

Keith, for instance, was correct to stand as a pastor for the sacredness of marriage. His idealism, however, caused him to imply that he could minister fully only to individuals who kept God's standard as completely as he believed it should be kept. In refusing to remarry "improper" divorcees, his implied message was, "Sorry, but you're too much of a sinner; you have to be purer for me to work with you." Did he believe that if he spoke God's truth often enough he would be able to erase ugly reality from his congregations? Did he believe that when people fall short of God's standards it is necessary to withdraw his blessing even if those imperfect sinners are trying to get their lives back on track?

It is both good and necessary to have ideal standards to guide Christians toward a life of fulfillment as long as it does not create blindness regarding reality. It is an undesirable reality that some marriages will disintegrate. It is also reality that people who have been through divorce can look back on their mistakes and learn to make improvements. In making these improvements, they may decide to remarry under something less than the ideal circumstances of Jesus' perfect principles. The pathway of grace is not perfect for these people, but instead of scorning them let's celebrate the fact that growth and healing are happening.

Judgmental People Are Fixed on Concrete Thinking

When was the last time you discussed an important topic with a child? In speaking with toddlers and early grade school children, you are rarely able to explore matters on a deep, abstract level. Children are very concrete in their thinking, as they tend to look at the world from a black-or-white frame of reference. If you ask a seven-year-old to say why he should not hit his younger sister, you will probably hear something like "Because you're not supposed to," or "Because I'll get in trouble," or "Because hitting is not nice." It would be rare indeed for a seven-year-old to discuss how love is a much higher priority in life and how aggression detracts from the communication of love. That line of reasoning would be too abstract for a seven-year-old child.

Once children enter adolescence, their capacity for abstract thinking increases greatly, and by early adulthood it should be sufficiently strong that it is much more powerful than merely appealing to concrete regulations. With abstract thinking comes freedom to explore ideas in a stimulating and purposeful manner. When exploring the deeper questions about relationships, God, or emotional issues, it is now less appropriate to refer only to the most elementary supposed-tos or had-betters. In adult thinking, concreteness gives way to higher reason and more searching thoughts.

Many adults, however, remain stuck in concrete patterns of thinking to the extent that they seem almost threatened by the privilege to set aside musts in order to more deeply pursue life with freedom of thought leading the way. One person put it to me this way: "If we encourage people to set aside the Bible's have-tos and let them think more broadly, who knows what heresy might result?" It never dawned on this person to say, "Who knows what kind of rich meaning spiritual people might find?"

Strict interpreters cling to their unbending, defensive position. They have not been fully challenged to move beyond their preadolescent approach to life. Their approach to decision making can be summarized by a bumper sticker: "The Bible says it, so that settles it." Additionally, they fundamentally are not willing to struggle with questions that do not fit easily into a fixed answer. As an example, most squirm when I ask them, "If a wife is in a physically abusive relationship with a Christian husband who has never committed adultery, are you suggesting that she should remain in that unhealthy state?" Most will concede, "This might be a time when separation is warranted." When I remind them that a high percentage of those separations end in divorce, they usually are stumped because they can't permit that possibility; yet only the most stubborn would encourage remaining in abuse.

Concrete thinkers rarely know what to do with questions that do not neatly fit into their simple paradigms. Though it is abundantly clear that gray circumstances cannot be ignored, they keep going back to the thought that says, "Yeah, but the rule is . . ." This form of thinking almost always originates in one's teen years, when choice-based thinking is rarely encouraged. They are merely superimposing their underdeveloped thought processes upon their theology.

Judgmental People Are Pain Avoiders

A major reason some people persist in their concrete notions is that concrete answers feel comfortable and secure. Once we say "This is the way it is and that's that," we are not required to confront the painful truth that our world virtually never fits into a "that's the way it is" model.

In Keith's earlier years of ministry, it was painful for him to minister to divorcees who could not or did not fit their lives into his prescribed regimen. Sin, imperfection, and missed opportunities are ugly!

Through his actions, he repeatedly communicated to people who had not been properly divorced that he would rather remove himself from their imperfections than run the risk of showing grace by re-marrying them. Offering grace would require him to feel the pain of their failure with them, and to agonize with them about how to proceed in a life that would never again meet God's perfect ideal for marriage. Rather than communicating that he was willing to help them build a new marriage on godly principles, his response was to hunker down in his own comfort zone, where he could not be compromised or criticized.

When I speak with new divorcees, whether they did or did not divorce for biblical reasons, one thing is consistent: they are in a time of personal trauma that can bring out such uncomfortable emotions as insecurity, anger, embarrassment, guilt, and loneliness. More than ever, these people need someone to put an arm around their shoulder and say, "I'll love you and work with you regardless of your flaws. You're worth the effort."

One pastor, Don, exemplified how Christians can take a *positive* approach with a person who has fallen short of the perfect biblical principles for marriage. For four years Don watched a woman in his church, Danielle, handle the stress of being a single mom with two teenagers. Her divorce came as a surprise to many because no one suspected that she and her former husband were having problems. In the early days after the divorce, it was rumored that Danielle had suffered some sort of emotional breakdown, perhaps a bad case of depression or anxiety. But lately she seemed to have weathered the storm and she was doing fine.

Each year, Don's church sponsored a special discipleship week-end for its high school students, where lifestyle issues and Christian values were emphasized. Many parents had to be recruited to be small group leaders and Danielle's name surfaced as one who could do the job.

When the pastor questioned her about her willingness to take a leadership role with the discipleship team, Danielle was hesitant because she knew some of the other parents might not want to set up a divorced woman as a role model for kids being taught Christian values. Hearing her reservations, Don looked squarely at her and said, "I know you've had troubles in the past and that you have pain regarding your mistakes, and that is precisely why I know you can be effective as you serve the Lord. When individuals hurt like you've hurt, it can't help but cause them to be more dependent than ever on God's empowerment, because when you feel weak, God is all you have left." Then continuing his challenge, Don said, "I want you to use your broken experience to help others avoid similar pitfalls. God will take your past and make it work in His favor."

Rather than avoiding the pain that Danielle had experienced, this pastor rightly jumped into her pain with both feet, saying, "I'm in there with you." He was emulating Christ!

Even the most shallow review of scripture uncovers the fact that God did not discard men or women once He saw that they had failed Him, sometimes miserably. Knowing that people can continue to be effective *especially* after pain, He built great ministries upon the shoulders of many a frail person. If it could happen in biblical days, could it not happen now?

Some, however, run from divorced Christians who are in pain. "Leave me out of it" is their message. "Your life is too crumpled and I don't want to leave my comfort zone to minister to you." Knowing they may have to encounter subjects (such as remarriage) that could evoke criticism from fellow judgmental people, they avoid those who would pull them into what they perceive as hot water if they appear too friendly.

This mind-set is not equipped to handle situations that are not mentioned in scripture, or that call for a more complicated resolution. Remember, Jesus did not stone the woman caught in adultery; nor did He always keep the Sabbath. He healed on the Sabbath, He touched lepers, and He forgave His lying friend, Peter. He encouraged the adulterous woman to get on with her life, but to sin no more. He examined Peter's heart and then blessed him with the care of His sheep. He recognized the failure and then graciously moved these broken people into restored and productive lives for Him. How could the abusive, murderous Saul become the brilliant and dedicated apostle Paul? Or the adulterous David continue to rule God's chosen people? Moses murdered a man in a fit of rage, but years later he became the great spiritual leader of God's chosen race.

Rather than avoiding the painful reality of sin and imperfection in the lives of His beloved, the Lord has a deep track record of taking people at their most painful place and saying, "I can still do business with you."

Judgment Props Up False Superiority

Every person begins life with an ability to feel inferior. Small children learn quickly that there are big people in their world called adults who get to call the shots. Daily they are reminded that those big people have the power that they can only wish to have. Likewise, as they mingle with peers in the school years, they learn that life consists of a pecking order based on criteria such as looks, social skills, grades, and athletic abilities. Children can be painfully aware of their comparative deficiencies, so they go to great lengths to emphasize their good points while covering the bad. Adding to this struggle with inferiority, they are guilty of doing things wrong, missing the standards, or embarrassing themselves with poor choices. It is a certainty that every developing person suffers in one way or another with some amount of inferiority.

People differ in how they learn to manage their inferiority feelings. Some collapse under the burden of their imperfections and too willingly accept lowliness as a way of life. These are the people who apologize too easily, who cling to guilt beyond its reasonable measure, or who are too eager to appease.

Others, however, respond to their inferiority feelings by gravitating toward behavior and attitudes that portray them to be superior. They reason that if they can find an angle that allows them to be in a one-up position, they have successfully overcome the possibility of being deemed inferior. It is this reasoning that pushes people to be condescending, to be perfectionistic, to focus on high achievement, or to invalidate differing opinions. Such behaviors can relieve individuals of feelings of lowliness, but the relief is only temporary because it does not adequately address the problem of inferiority.

Christian doctrine gives us a fixed remedy for the problem of inferiority, and it is not anchored in a strategy to become superior. Deep down, any person who contemplates the need for spiritual vitality recognizes that "all have sinned and have fallen short of the glory of God." Before God, we each stand as inferior beings. We have no right to march into heaven's throne room, high-fiving saints and angels along the way and then presenting ourselves to God with an attitude that implies, "Aren't you lucky to have me here with you?" Our sinfulness is so thorough, so persistent, that any honest person is forced to admit that we indeed are inadequate as we present ourselves to God.

It is the atoning death of Jesus Christ (and nothing else) that has redeemed us from our place of inferiority. As we claim His righteousness as a covering for our own inadequacies, we indeed are privileged to relate with God in the comfort of knowing that He loves us dearly and He dismisses all references to our pitiable state. With Christ as our defender, no inferiority struggles need to persist. We are judged worthy and righteous in Him.

Most Christians are quite familiar with the doctrine of humankind's innate, sinful nature and the doctrine of Christ's atonement on behalf of individuals who call on Him to be their bridge to God. Despite this realization, some make the mistake of assuming, "I'd better make sure that I'm always going to be acceptable to God, so for good measure I will perform in a way that shows that I am not of inferior stock, and if I encounter people along the way who are missing God's perfect mark, I'll make it my job to set them straight."

Overlooking the ongoing evidence of their own innate inadequacy, they zero in on pet subjects (divorce being one of them) that they can champion. Virtually always they deny the fact that they are trying to appear superior, stating, "I'm not at all holding myself up as better than anyone else. I'm simply trying to be loyal to the truth of God." Though loyalty to God's truth is both wise and noble, these people portray their true spirit in refusing to have full fellowship with those who differ, even when the erring ones are attempting to reconnect with a life of godliness.

Perhaps you have heard the saying, "The ground is level at the foot of the cross." No one appealing to the grace of God has the prerogative to hold himself or herself above another. There *are* times when it is necessary to detach from people who blatantly mock the principles of scripture and God, but this detachment is certainly not warranted in most divorce cases. Christian divorcees have failed to maintain a viable marriage, but most desire to continue in personal growth and their walk with the Lord. They are no different from non-divorced Christians who also are imperfect but desiring to continue to grow. Those who cannot acknowledge the equal need for God's grace amid their human frailty are not simply being true to God's standards; they are attempting to compensate for their own sinfulness by falsely assuming they are on higher ground than someone else. This false smugness is most undesirable since it blinds them to the fact that we are each equally loved by God.

Judgmental People Forget the Primacy of Love

A friend of mine has a plaque on his desk that reads, "Things are not essential to success." For years, this man has made it his mission to reach out to the disenfranchised, the hurting, the underdog. His reputation is impeccable, as he is known widely to be a man of goodness, kindness, and encouragement. When he hears of someone who has fallen or is troubled, his first reaction is not to assess blame but to ask, "How can I be of help?" He knows people are fragile and prone to mistakes, so he is keenly aware that he is often able to be a positive presence in many lives as he remains vigilant regarding how God can use him next.

Sadly, the more focused we are in maintaining correctness, the less we are capable of responding to imperfection with the loving spirit demonstrated by my friend. As Keith explained, "In years past, when a couple in my congregation was divorcing, my first concern was to find out who was at fault. Once that was determined, then I could decide who deserved my kindness and who deserved my confrontation."

When a couple divorces, there is always the possibility that one partner has acted out more overtly than the other. Surely you have heard comments like these:

- "My understanding is that he became very interested in a woman at work and that's what caused them to separate."
- "The word is out that she was a mean woman that no one could live with."
- "I'm pretty sure he was physically abusive, or at least he had a really bad temper."

What's behind such statements? Usually, dissecting a couple's divorce is done for the purpose of measuring blame. Once the person most at fault is determined, sides are then chosen and one spouse is supported while the other is shunned.

Indeed, there are times when it is appropriate for friends and acquaintances to determine the factors that led to the eventual decision to divorce. Certainly in my counseling role, I am in an ongoing process of assessing wrongs; however, I try not to assess for the purpose of blaming, but rather for the purpose of learning how better to love and heal.

Many say, "But when a person seeks a divorce that is driven by poor priorities, they need to be confronted." Perhaps so, but the real question is, "In what manner and for what purpose should we confront?" Too many people confront for the purpose of setting others right (translated: "Make them live according to my rules") and generally their method of confrontation is condescending. Grace-oriented people confront in order to clear the way for a deeper exchange of love.

An example is Allison, who was confronted by an elder in her church because she had filed divorce papers though there was no affair or abandonment. Her reason for divorcing was that her husband had "resigned" his role in the home. In her words, "he just quit and was completely detached from the kids and me." The elder told Allison, "I'm sure you've got your reasons for wanting to move away from him, but the church needs to stand up for the sacredness of marriage. At some point, we've all got to learn to live with things that don't go our way."

Hurt by the elder's unwillingness to understand her futility at home, she turned away from him and the church altogether. Two or three years later, she finally began attending church again, but this time she was met by a pastor who told her, "When someone divorces it usually means that there has been a lot of pain for a long time. Please let us know when you are hurting; don't keep your pain hidden like you have in the past. You're among friends here, and you'll need to be reminded often of the enormousness of God's love for you."

Knowledge and correctness are good and necessary qualities to honor, but some people's zeal can be so fixed on what is right that they forget how Christ came to love and minister to individuals fully aware that they would never perfect the manner of life He taught. Even though it is honorable that they seek to please God with their witness (just as the Pharisees believed they too were pleasing God), they could be more effective in their witness if they did as Jesus did when He stated, "It is not those who are healthy who need a physician, but those who are sick. But go and learn what this means, 'I desire compassion and not sacrifice,' for I did not come to call the righteous, but sinners" (Matthew 9:12–13).

Judgment Implies Forgetfulness

One of my fantasies is to go back in time to conduct a long interview with the apostle Paul. Primarily, I'd like to get biographical information first, and then I'd begin injecting philosophical questions. It would be fascinating to hear him recount how his childhood and early adult years unfolded, and to have him talk with me about how his Pharisaical life influenced his emotions, his relationships, and his view of God. Then I would like to hear him contrast his early life as a Pharisee with his later life as a born-again Christian. At the top of my list of queries would be a question about the doctrine of grace and how it changed his understanding of himself, his relational style with others, and his relationship with God.

I picture Paul being gleeful as he discusses grace with me in this fantasy conversation. I also imagine him referring often to the times in his Pharisaical past when he clearly missed the meaning of God's message for humanity. In his biblical writings, he is not at all bashful in describing himself as the chief of sinners, as weak, or as foolish. At the base of his love for grace is a deep and reverent appreciation for the fact that he lived in spiritual bankruptcy before he finally encountered the breadth of the love God felt for him.

Though Paul has been gone for almost two millennia, he has left us with his own reflections regarding the grace of God, as recorded in his writings. It is no exaggeration to state that his understanding of it grew in direct proportion to the realization of his spiritual brokenness outside God's presence. This same sense of brokenness is missing for many Christians today.

Ask Christian divorcees who practice their faith today if they know what spiritual brokenness feels like, and most will nod their heads and say emphatically, "Oh, yes. I know what it's like to feel broken, and let me tell you, it's not at all fun." Most can recount feelings of self-doubt, humiliation, disillusionment, futility, or emptiness. They will tell you that divorce is a painful reminder that no matter how well intended they are capable of making poor decisions, or that they can mismanage their emotions and relational skills. It is difficult to be a prideful divorcee.

Now, shift gears and ask some modern keepers of the Law (particularly ones who have not been divorced) if they also know what spiritual brokenness feels like; the responses are likely to sound different. Most will state that they know how brokenness and contrition are necessary ingredients for the Christian walk, but (at least this is my experience) they will not speak with the same emotional pitch as those whose failures are exposed for all to see. The subject of brokenness can be intellectualized just like any other doctrine, but it does not have a powerful effect on people's lifestyles until it can be embraced for what it is, a truly mind-altering experience.

Keith put it this way: "You have to understand that Monica has been my pride and joy since the day she was born. I cannot recall one single day when I wouldn't willingly lay down my life for her if it were necessary. She means that much to me. When she got divorced, I was devastated for one reason and one reason alone: I hated seeing her in so much pain. She's become a fine young woman who deserves the best. Is she perfect? Well, no not really. But she'll always be my little girl who deserves all the love I can give her."

Then Keith paused as he reflected, "Monica is an extension of me. Whatever frailties she possesses, she has them in part because she's my daughter. It was in the aftermath of her failure that I truly came to terms with the need for God's grace, both in her life and in mine. For years, I had been teaching the necessity of upholding the sacredness of marriage. However, as I put myself in Monica's shoes, I realized that I had seen myself as set apart from those people I quietly considered to be failures. But the realization hit me like a lightning bolt. If Monica was a failure, which she was, then I was a failure too! Somewhere along the line, I had not provided perfectly for her, I had misread signs, or I had not met her needs completely. She needed God's grace because she was now certifiably imperfect, but the same could be said of me!"

Keith's transformation is one that many could share. It is good that we learn the truth about God's ideals, but we can simultaneously recognize that we all need God's compassion. We are not compromising godly principles to continue in full fellowship with those who have failed. Rather, our ongoing support serves as a reminder that we are all nothing more than broken shards of clay whose lives have been mended by the Master Craftsman. He chooses not to let any remain in a state of defeat. Like Keith, recognition of each person's broken state is empty if it is mere intellectualization. It has to be personalized, and in most cases it is best accompanied through a sense of agony as the full measure of personal sinfulness is acknowledged.

When people choose to judge divorcees for their marital failure, the judgment speaks volumes regarding their own inability to appreciate their own utterly broken state when they were first given the gift of God's grace. As a contrast, by entering into a healing relationship with those who have fallen short, we illustrate an abiding appreciation for the beautiful truth that God's love is the ultimate gift that sets the stage for restoration.

Chapter Twelve

Glue for Broken Marriages

Anyone who works with divorcees repeatedly encounters situations where the puzzle of how to hold a marriage together is still unsolved. I often speak with husbands and wives who are trying to decide if they should continue together or make the split permanent. Sometimes a major trauma, such as an affair, has caused them to examine the viability of the relationship. Other couples admit that they have ceased liking each other, or that character flaws have become so prominent that they feel futile in dealing with each other. Yet even where a couple is contemplating divorce, I often find that under all the hurt, anger, and disillusionment the candle of love has not been completely snuffed out. If that is the case, it is wisest to first proceed with the couple in the hope of rekindling the relationship. I tell couples that love can actually be strengthened by facing major hurts and confronting the issues that have not been fully resolved.

For instance, one couple, whom we'll call Jodi and Patrick, had a major blow-up that resulted in the police being called to the house and Patrick being arrested. The foul after-effect lasted several months because the incident brought to light how anger had been too dominant in their lives for too long. Shortly after the argument, Jodi was ready to file for divorce and put an end to the couple's twenty-year marriage. But before doing so, she wisely decided to seek counseling.

As she spoke with me about her life with Patrick, it was clear that their marriage had not always been bad. Though there were numerous incidents of angry flare-ups, there were also many times marked by kindness and togetherness. The couple had two teenaged daughters who were heavily involved in school and church activities, and though they disliked the arguments between their parents it seemed clear that they would be powerfully affected if a divorce occurred. Jodi would have to go back to work, and the girls would be on their own too much; neither parent wanted to put the girls at risk for problems.

Talking with people like Jodi and Patrick, I tell them: "Ten years from now, as you look back on this time of difficulty, I'd rather you regret that you tried too hard to keep the marriage afloat as opposed to choosing a hasty divorce. Now is a time when you can make some major adjustments in your relationship if you're truly serious about change. Strange but true, people make their greatest relational improvements not when things are going well but when things seem to have fallen apart."

Keys to Avoiding Divorce

Talking with couples about the viability of their marriage, one sees several key factors that need to be carefully weighed. Rather than too quickly opting for divorce, it is wise to assess if the right ingredients can be put into play in order to build a more peaceful union. Let's examine some of those key factors.

Internal Factors Are Given Highest Priority

Do you know the most frequently used word in marital arguments? Very simply, it's *you*. A couple experiencing peak marital frustration inevitably goes into a blaming, accusing style of interaction. They do so because the *you* approach to problem solving actually indicates a form of emotional laziness. The implication is, "If I could just get other people to act correctly, then I'd be fine in how I handle my problems." The weakness of this approach is that most spouses do not like being given the responsibility for the other's emotional well-being. Usually, they have several counteraccusations to hurl right back.

Couples habitually engaging in the blaming pattern indicate on a deeper level that they are letting their dependencies play too prominent a role. Dependency can be defined as allowing your mood or your inner sense of direction to be determined by external factors. It is often not part of a person's conscious awareness; nonetheless, it is still a powerful influence over how problems are addressed. My desire, as a counselor, is to help couples see the distasteful results of excessive dependency so they become less externally focused and more internally focused in their problem-solving efforts.

Let's first acknowledge that this emotional dependency is not entirely wrong. In His ingenious design, God created each individual with a hunger to be loved, a desire for affirmation. With this ingredient in place, individuals naturally seek refuge from complete isolation, looking toward others for fellowship and nurturing, and that is good. For instance, by speaking words of encouragement couples lift each other's mood. Likewise, if they can laugh with each other or console one another after a difficult event, this is a positive form of dependency. By upholding one another, they enhance each other's quality of life.

Problems arise, however, when there is an imbalance in the forms of a couple's dependencies. For instance, husbands and wives who become aggressively angry because the other has failed to act as expected suggest an imbalance. It is as if one is saying to the other, "I'm putting you in charge of making me feel good about myself, and I cannot rest until I get the right response." Quietly, the spouse has conceded that in the absence of the other's ideal behavior, he or she is unable to maintain emotional composure. Sometimes spouses give up on relationships altogether and go into a major withdrawal. More often, however, they look to the mate, insisting that he or she should provide emotional nourishment. Communication becomes forced, and angry debates can erupt.

I explain to couples that it *is* legitimate to spell out their needs to each other. Since God does not expect marital partners to live in an emotional desert, it is reasonable to hope for some healthy nurturing. Speaking the truth in love to each other, they can enter into a "coaching communication," where they teach each other how to know and respond to one another's personalities. Healthy relationships make room for this form of interaction. For example, it is fair for a wife to tell her husband how she would prefer him to coordinate his schedule with hers; it is reasonable for a husband to discuss with his wife how he wants her to have patience when he feels stressed because of an unusual work deadline.

When it becomes clear that the spouse is not receptive to constructive coaching, many marriage partners make the mistake of increasing their level of emotional intensity by trying to persuade, or by using manipulative techniques such as the silent treatment. In an effort to have their dependency needs satisfied, they lose sight of the fact that they are moving toward disaster. Spouses complain to me frequently that no matter how many times they try to express their needs, the partner just won't catch on; they then rationalize why they must persist with coercive or manipulative communication. My response is to challenge these people to accept reality and try another path to personal fulfillment.

The path that I encourage is the internal path. Rather than insist that their external world must conform to their specific expectations, they can learn to find contentment even if the partner is not synchronized with their efforts. The apostle Paul wrote in Philippians 4:11, "I have learned to be content in whatever circumstances I am." To be sure, this is not an easy task; even so, it is attainable.

As I spoke with Jodi and Patrick about the anger episode that caused her to call the police, I asked them to identify the legitimate needs they were wanting the other to address at that moment. The gist of their responses was that they each wanted to be respected and know that the other would take the time to contemplate what each was asking of the other.

That seemed fair to me. Next, I asked them each to determine the point where one or both crossed the line in their thinking, becoming convinced that they absolutely had to have the other's concurrence in order to maintain emotional composure. Patrick told me his line was crossed when Jodi indicated that she didn't care how he felt. At that moment, he got so angry that he just kept insisting on his way. Jodi told me her line was crossed when Patrick became so angry. At that moment, she became convinced that she could no longer be civil if he would not be civil. I explained to them that their reactions represented normal dependency that had gone too far. Whether consciously aware of it or not, they were each convinced that the other *must* act right in order for personal calmness to be maintained. This is when the blaming and accusing began to crescendo.

As we examined this incident, we then put it into the overall backdrop of their communication patterns of the preceding twenty years. It was easy for them to determine that this dependency imbalance (which played out in coercive communication) was a fixture in their relationship from the very beginning. Both admitted being unnecessarily pushy and insistent about how they expected the other to think and act. I explained that they could continue in their habit of trying to control each other in an effort to find personal peace; that would always be an option. But as they examined the reality of expecting to find the same lousy consequences each time they let their dependencies run amok, they determined that a whole new mind-set was desirable.

The better path to peace, I explained, is to emphasize the spiritual ingredients that constitute a contented life. Rather than looking to one another to be the ultimate providers of contentment, it would be best to make room for the reality that the other can and will fail. On the other hand, drawing upon God's guidance and strength, they could maintain composure even if the other was a disappointment.

In explaining this concept to Jodi and Patrick, I asked each to determine the traits they believed God wanted them to emphasize in their roles as wife and husband. They each gave similar answers, stating that they believed the Lord would have them live with patience, understanding, kindness, respect, encouragement, and self-restraint. I then asked if they could pinpoint common moments when they pressed each other to act right so they could get on with their effort to have those desirable traits. They each had no problem identifying moments when they did so. Then I asked them to consider an alternative. Instead of trying to rearrange each other's attitudes and behaviors, I challenged them to commit to God that they would give one another patience and understanding (and so forth) *knowing* the other was in a disagreeable mind-set. In other words, they would choose to let God guide their attitudes (be internally focused) instead of forcing another human to set the tone for the right attitudes (being externally focused).

It is not easy to shift gears mentally after you have operated in one mode for years; but it can be done. As soon as it becomes apparent that couples are willing to take personal responsibility for their actions as opposed to blaming, I grow increasingly confident that the marriage can be saved. Conversely, couples giving only lip service to the notion of letting God be their guide quickly resort to blaming and control; the possibility of marital healing remains low. The refusal to operate with right introspection is most assuredly an indication of the hardened heart that Jesus referred to in Matthew 19:8 (more on that later in this chapter).

Acceptance Can Be Restructured

In the early stages of most marriages, couples easily express love and acceptance. They are brimming with optimism, on their best behavior, and assuming positive qualities in each other even when blunders occur or past mistakes are revealed. The nature of young love is to forgive easily and to give the benefit of the doubt whenever needed.

As time passes, though, so can the cheery optimism. Reality hits home as each partner is forced to realize that the other's quirks not only don't go away but keep recurring despite hopes to the contrary. With human nature being heavily directed by self-absorption, it is a certainty that partners will at times be insensitive, impatient, unaware, or emotionally erratic.

With the growing realization of ongoing flaws in the marriage, it is possible to truly determine just how successful the marriage can be. Those who are able to openly accept each other, even as it is clear that imperfections will continue, have the greatest chance of finding the soul ties that produce lasting relational contentment. Those who cannot accept ongoing imperfection but instead wish to restructure the other's personality find marriage to be displeasing and difficult.

Jodi and Patrick could easily look back and recognize their shift from a high level of acceptance to low. Jodi explained: "When Patrick and I dated, he was the perfect gentleman. He always treated me respectfully, and I never heard him say a cross word to me or anyone else. We often had long talks about our beliefs, our dreams, our past mistakes, and our future intentions. Communication was deep and rewarding."

Patrick chimed in. "I was never what you would call a deep communicator until Jodi came along. My family had a habit of holding things inside, and the idea of having a heart-to-heart talk about *anything* was nonexistent. When she started pulling personal things out of me, it was really different and I realized we had something special that I really needed."

My question was, "So when did things take a turn in the wrong direction?"

Jodi explained. "Within the first year it became clear to me that Patrick wasn't nearly as interested in personal sharing as when we dated. I was amazed at how he would ignore me or show irritability in ways that I had not seen before. I would try to talk with him about my frustration but he would lash out at me, letting me know my perception was way off."

"That's not at all the way I see it," came his retort. "I've always been willing to talk with my wife about what I think and feel, but she has *got* to be one of the most defensive people I've ever known. If I tell her anything that just barely hints at a disagreement, she gets huffy and accuses me of being irrational. We've had hundreds of little arguments over the years that could have easily been avoided if she weren't so quick to criticize me or invalidate what I have to say. If she says I've become more guarded or less open, it's true, but only because I have deliberately chosen not to put myself on the line, knowing she's just going to start chopping away at my character."

If I had let them, Patrick and Jodi would have gone on and on, hacking away at the deficiencies they saw in each other. By this time in their relationship, neither was bashful at reminding the other of what he or she did not like. I have learned that couples who are on the brink of divorce, as this couple was, have long since lost the willingness to put their best foot forward or to see each other in the ideal fashion of their distant past. Instead, their former optimism is supplanted by a low level of tolerance of the humanness they once were able to accept in each other.

It is easy to display acceptance for someone who happens to think and act just as you want. The mark of maturity, though, is to accept others when it is clear that differences are ongoing. In counseling, Jodi and Patrick came to realize that their verbal sniping at one another was an indication of their lack of acceptance.

To have this couple reassess their capacity to accept each other, I asked them first to list verbally several things about one another they did not like. Jodi said that Patrick spoke too harshly during disagreements, and often his timing was poor. Likewise, he had a habit of not finishing projects he'd started, and he displayed a critical spirit whenever others did not conform to his exacting standards. For his part, Patrick said Jodi had a difficult time admitting wrongs, was often late, left junk all over the house, and could be aloof and unaffectionate. They each could have listed more complaints, but they were satisfied they had identified the major ones.

After they articulated their dislikes, I asked both of them to picture what their response to the other would be like if they chose to display acceptance toward those undesirable features. Neither liked my idea, but Patrick got the ball rolling as he replied, "You mean, if Jodi leaves shoes in the living room or if she lets several days of junk mail sit on the kitchen table, I should just shake it off and not worry about it?" I nodded agreement. "I *suppose* I could try that, although I wouldn't necessarily like it." Jodi too made a weak effort to respond to my challenge by suggesting she could let some of Patrick's critical comments pass without her having to correct each one, and maybe she could forgive him for being more impatient than she was.

Then I made my point. "There will always be reasons for you to confront each other about personal flaws, and sometimes it is both good and necessary. But I'm assuming that if I talked with you twenty years from now, there would still be imperfections in your life. So even as you commit to openly discussing problems constructively, you're going to need to make room for the reality that *some* crud will remain. No marriage is perfect."

I continued: "There is an arrogance on display whenever you refuse to accept each other as imperfect. You don't have the same flaws in your personalities, but you each have flaws. Just as you want to be accepted with all your humanness, it is fair to offer the same to one another."

I explain to couples like Jodi and Patrick that acceptance does not require them to merely suppress disgruntled feelings. There *are* times to be firm about core values and to establish reasonable boundaries. Likewise, though, it is good to know when not to pick battles that are not fruitful.

The key to true acceptance of each other is trust. Couples concur that although they may not like certain aspects of one another's personalities this does not mean they are evil at heart or truly malicious in intent. They may see one another as sometimes misguided, but that is not the same as untrustworthy. For instance, one wife told me, "Sometimes my husband pops off with sharp opinions about the way people ought to be, and that's a quality in him that I wish would go away. Years ago, I'd try to correct him every time he spouted his unnecessary opinions. Now, though, I just accept the fact that he's just that way. I'm not required to agree with him; nor do I always remain silent. But over the years, I've realized that despite this flaw, he's also got plenty of good qualities. I trust him overall because even with his hard-headedness, he's still a decent man."

Acceptance does not require ceasing all confrontation. Sometimes we need to "be angry without sin" and to "speak the truth in love" (Ephesians 4:26, 15). It does, however, imply that we drop idealism. No marriage partner will ever be what you want, so you need to factor that reality in, sometimes more often than you might like.

If you honestly cannot say that you trust the character of your spouse and that acceptance would lead to disastrous results, you may be in a toxic relationship that cannot continue. Before drawing such a conclusion, though, be willing to consider expanding your acceptance range.

Hardness of Heart

In determining if a marriage can be saved, another criterion to examine is the extent of a partner's hardened heart. Sometimes a spouse sits in my office speaking with great exasperation about the mate's total unwillingness to live in a loving manner. "I have tried every way I know to be appropriate," the person claims, "but it makes no difference how good I am or how often I attempt to engage my spouse in a meaningful way; our marriage remains headed toward disaster." In such a case, it could be that an irreversible hardness of heart has settled into the spouse.

When Jesus referred to "hardness of heart" as the reason for the Mosaic law of divorce, He did not specify exactly what that phrase meant. He did seem to imply that marital partners can sometimes be so unwilling to live in accordance with biblical common sense that continuing the marital union may be virtually impossible. Our task is to find a fair understanding of His words so that in some of today's troubled marriages reasonable decisions can be made.

Though not scientifically or exhaustively, I have observed several qualities in partners who demonstrate a thorough inability to live within the realm of reasonableness. Judge for yourself to determine if these traits are consistent with a hardened heart:

- A strong need to be in control. (A controlling spirit plays right into Satan's hands, as it is his desire to remain outside the control of God's will by playing God himself.)

- A spirit of meanness, typified by caustic criticism and a refusal to forgive.

- Major mismanagement of anger. This could be displayed in rage or a chronic pattern of passive-aggressive anger such as persistent withdrawal.

- A tendency to lead so strongly with irrational emotions such as fretting and agitation that logic and reason have no place.

- Gross neglect of fundamental family needs, and unwillingness to participate in the functions of a family, even at the most basic level.

- Chronic insensitivity, where the spouse seems unable to factor in the other's legitimate needs or feelings.

- A haughty, prideful spirit, as typified by a destructive, condescending nature and inability to correct wrongs, particularly if it perpetuates ongoing pain.

- Spiritual disengagement, especially to the extent of being openly antagonistic to accountability before the Lord for personal growth.

- Ongoing deception, pathological lying, and manipulative behavior, especially when they involve unethical or grossly irresponsible behavior.

- Unwillingness to adequately address addictions and substance abuse.

Other qualities could be mentioned, but in general hardness of heart represents a life that is defined by such self-absorption that the ability to love is almost completely lost.

I have encountered numerous marriages where great errors occurred, including lying, adultery, and wild anger. It is tempting to conclude in such a case that the marriage is over, but this is not always so. Sometimes the erring partner is remorseful and sufficiently willing to change that it would be a poor decision to divorce. Tremendous growth awaits a couple in the aftermath of wrong choices, so in many of these cases it is wise to encourage staying together.

On the other hand, I have encountered numerous marriages that did not involve the gross errors of adultery or physical abuse, but they offered little hope for ever producing a form of love that could sustain the long-term prospects of the marriage. In these cases, the erring spouse usually shows no willingness whatsoever to be loving and godly toward the mate, as if that person were in fact permanently committed to the unsettling behavior. In those instances, the hardness of heart may be so fixed that the partner has no hope of ever experiencing a vibrant, God-honoring relationship. The partner might stay in such a toxic relationship and develop traits that become increasingly unhealthy with the passing of time.

I encourage couples who might be considering divorce to continue their efforts to stay together if there is evidence that hardness of heart is not yet entrenched. No matter how difficult the problems may have been, if approached with a learning spirit there is a high potential that love can be not only reestablished but enhanced because of the effort. Only where there is ungodly behavior and a thorough unwillingness to change is it reasonable to consider separation. The marriage commitment is so desirable that it deserves the most powerful effort. Even if hardness of heart seems fixed, there is still another significant issue to consider before divorce might be pursued: the children.

The Children's Needs

In a high percentage of divorces, children are involved, and their presence makes the determination for divorce a much more serious matter since it is likely that they will be the ones to pay the highest emotional price. I often hear couples state, "If it weren't for the kids, we would already be divorced by now." Of course, such a statement is null and void even as the words proceed from a couple's mouths since it represents a circumstance that does not exist. There *are* children involved, so it is pointless to discuss what would be done if they were not there.

Jodi and Patrick's children were sixteen and thirteen. Each represented a whole separate set of needs that could not be ignored. The older daughter was just beginning to date, and the parents wanted her to see a healthy example of male-female relating. The younger daughter had lots of issues with anger and insecurity, which would predictably intensify if her parents split.

As the couple contemplated the potential consequences of divorce, they both concluded that the children would be thrown into such emotional confusion as to produce predictably grave results. "We chose to have these children," Patrick reminded himself, "and they are not an accident. Since they are God's gift to us, and we have been entrusted with their care, it would be wrong to give them anything but our best." They rightly concluded that since they had two extra pairs of eyes watching their every move, they had the highest motivation to exchange anger for respect, control for freedom, and defensiveness for openness. "If we cut and run from this marriage," Patrick concluded, "without addressing our core flaws, we will both probably wind up in another marriage that produces the same results. Then the pain our kids experienced will be even worse." This couple was wisely putting their decision into the broader perspective, and they determined together there was much to be gained by exercising self-restraint and much to lose if they merely proceeded with the same old patterns in play.

Patrick and Jodi's case can be contrasted with a situation presented by Stephanie, a woman in her late thirties and married twelve years who had a ten-year-old son and eight-year-old daughter. "When we were first married, Kent surprised me when he told me he hoped we would not have children. Because that thinking was so foreign to me, I didn't even address it when we were dating. I just assumed we would have kids. Well, I prevailed upon him to succumb to my desire to have children, but sure enough, he's had very little to do with them. He didn't change one diaper when they were infants. I never left either child with him alone because he said he didn't want to baby-sit. When I tried to explain that being a dad is not the same as being a baby-sitter, he honestly did not comprehend what I was saying."

Stephanie went on to explain that Kent basically lived his life with virtually no regard for her needs or those of the children. He rarely yelled, though he was often grumpy. He simply chose not to participate in their lives, preferring instead to work late during the week and play golf on as many weekend days as the weather would allow. He bought no Christmas presents or birthday gifts, and rarely did they ever eat together as a foursome.

The children were now at an age where they asked her questions about their dad's behavior: "Why is Daddy never home?" "Is my Daddy mad at me?" "Brittany's dad goes to Indian Princess with her; why won't Daddy do that with me?" Because there were no good answers to such questions, Stephanie would try to appease the kids as quickly as possible and then divert their attention elsewhere.

In some cases, the relations with one parent may be so strained that it might be more harmful to the children for the parents to remain together. Sometimes, when parents are no longer burdened by daily aggravations with each other, the mother and father separately give the children messages of love and security that they could not communicate jointly. As I spoke with Stephanie, however, about her strains with Kent, we both concluded that it would likely be worse for her two children if they divorced, since it was highly probable that Kent might abandon his parental role completely if he lived as a single man. At least he came home in the evenings and the children could tell him about the day's events. He was not openly antagonistic, nor was he overtly mean. Though Stephanie did not like the role of being the go-between for her children and their father, at least she could arrange to have him do a few things each month that satisfied the kids' need for attention. She concluded that although she might feel relieved to have Kent permanently out of the house, her children would have even less time with him. Also, because she would have to return to work, their time with her would also be diminished. Stephanie chose to stay in the marriage, learning to internally manage her own hurts and disappointments, knowing that such a choice would be a worthy sacrifice for the young ones who depended so heavily on her to establish a peaceful home atmosphere.

I respect people like Stephanie who conclude that the children's needs should take priority over their own. My bias leans toward erring in the direction of maintaining the marriage if at all possible. At the same time, when people like Stephanie, Jodi, and Patrick tell me they've done all they can do to save a marriage but to no avail, I want to be known as loving even if they divorce. My hope is that they have been as wise and objective as possible in weighing their options, and I assume it is folly for me to say what the best decision ultimately would be since I have not lived in their circumstances for the same length of time.

Chapter Thirteen

Grace for All

In Matthew 20:1–16, Jesus tells the story of a landowner who hires laborers for his vineyard at the beginning of the day. As the day progresses, he brings in more laborers to complete the work. Some are hired at the third hour, some the sixth, and the ninth, and then finally at the eleventh hour. At the end of the day, each received the same wage, a denarius. The laborers who were hired early complained about the fact that those who had not worked as hard or produced as much received the same full day's wage. The gist of the landowner's reply was, "It's my money and I'll pay it out as I choose; but in the meantime, be happy that you received a fair wage."

This parable captures the difference between humans who keep score regarding righteousness and the Lord, who defies logic by showing goodness without regard for the scorecard. Jesus' message was, "No human has the right to tell God they are more deserving of His reward when compared to any other person. God is merciful and will love in a way that may never fit your logical schemes."

When I consider modern Christians who struggle to accept other Christians who have been divorced, I am struck by the parallels to this parable. They seem to imply, "I've lived a life that is honoring to God and my choices will stand the test of time. It is unfair that God would then give the same goodness to people who have not labored as faithfully as I. While I don't mind if God gives those divorced Christians *some* goodness, they should never be given as much as me."

Any judgment toward a person who has experienced a failed marriage (or two, three, or four) represents a form of scorekeeping that God does not honor. I *do* believe that it is wise for the church to become involved in the life of the one who has experienced failure in order to assist in healing and spiritual growth. I also believe that if it is apparent someone has not learned from failure and persists in destructive patterns of life, this should be taken as a signal that the person is probably not a good candidate for a role of leadership. I do *not* believe that Christians should turn their backs on these same people, though, especially if they show evidence that they want to continue in fellowship with believers who can help them stay on track in finding God. We should refrain from scorekeeping that causes some Christians to identify one group as winners and another group as losers.

As an example, Dennis was an active lay leader in his local church congregation. The ministerial staff found him to be a wise advisor on many subjects, and the church members knew him to be a knowledgeable teacher. Unfortunately, Dennis and his wife of many years divorced. Most people did not know the reasons for the divorce because the couple had wisely chosen to take the high road and not air their dirty laundry. His former wife moved to another part of the city, so Dennis remained at the church after becoming single. He and his pastor decided it would be good for him to take a break from his formal responsibilities at the church so he could heal and get back on track in his new circumstances.

After two years, some of the church members approached the pastor about having Dennis teach a Bible study class. The pastor said he could not support such an option; he cited James 3:1, "Let not many of you become teachers." Then he cited a portion of James 3:12, which says that a fig tree cannot produce olives and a vine cannot produce figs. He explained, "Dennis is still a good person, but his life has not produced the right fruit; so we cannot reward him any longer with a position of leadership." He clearly saw appointment to a teaching position as a reward for doing the right thing in his life.

Later, Dennis moved to another church and once again made good friends and began winning the confidence of the church members and the pastor. After time, the same scenario came about. He was asked if he would take a leadership position in one of the church's Bible study classes. Still smarting from his former pastor's rebuke, he declined. Later, he had a conversation with his new pastor, who spoke from another perspective. He said: "I'm sorry you have been divorced and I'm sure it is not what you wanted, but you need to know that we are not keeping score here. Taking a leadership position is not merely a payoff for doing things correctly. If God has gifted you to teach and if you're certain that you would be under God's leading in that role, it would be wrong for you *not* to follow His call. Yes, we would want you to represent the Lord well by maintaining right leadership characteristics. That part still matters. But the main thrust of my message to you is that I want you to have the liberty to respond to God's urging as you deem fit."

In the first church, responsibilities were handed out on the basis of performance criteria only. In the second church, there were also performance criteria (ability to teach, exhibiting godliness and leadership qualities), but the ultimate determinant for this man's church involvement was the call of God.

The Character of God

In getting away from a scorekeeping mentality in the church, we can change our understanding of God and His will for the life of each Christian. We can learn to see God as compassionate, comforting, generous, and more concerned with our spirit than with our résumés. Let's look at each of these qualities.

God's Compassion

Think about the many tasks you take on each week, and consider how central fulfillment of the task is to personal satisfaction. Your chores can be as simple as cleaning the kitchen sink or as complicated as open heart surgery. Once the task (no matter how large or small) is completed, you can feel a certain contentment as you survey your work and think, "Job well done."

As gratifying as task completion may be, it is nowhere near the most important quality in defining a life of success. Compassion, love, and kindness are the qualities central to the character of God; only if such qualities are central to you and me can we know that we have progressed in becoming Christlike.

Repeatedly I have heard stories from divorcees who recount how non-Christians were kind upon hearing the news of their divorce while Christians were anything but kind. It seems that those who do not have absolute standards of right and wrong can be more capable of being tender at a time when tenderness is needed, while those who stand for righteousness are more consumed with the standard (and its performance implications) than with the person.

Contrast the hard-nosed position with the compassion illustrated in the parable of the landowner who hired the laborers. Certainly he was concerned about performance; after all, he had a task he wanted done. The laborers were instructed what to do; then they were supervised as they did their work. We should take note of the fact that those hired near the end of the day were probably men who were down on their luck, struggling to keep up their feelings of adequacy because of their poor lot in life. When the time came to pay wages, the amount given was not determined entirely by the work completed. (Their work was *a* factor in that they had to be in the vineyards before he gave them compensation.) Rather, the wage was more of a function of the landowner's compassion. He chose to treat those who did not perform fully just as he would treat those who labored the maximum amount. Why? His compassion compelled him to do so.

Today's Christians can be so consumed with the accuracy with which a person keeps God's perfect standards that they forget to apply God's perfect compassion. Dennis, for instance, missed the mark in living according to the fullest Christian standard, as evidenced by the fact that he was divorced. One church chose not to treat him with compassion, while another gave him the message, "We want you to feel that you belong here, and that God can use your gifts and talents here." They recognized his *marriage* as a failure, not Dennis himself as a failure.

Any of God's attention, whether or not we have been divorced, comes from His attitude of compassion. Knowing fully that we deserve no goodness at all from Him, God nonetheless wants to express His care by using us for His service despite the deficiencies we each bring. Rather than giving highest priority to strict justice, His thoughts are more oriented toward fulfilling the individual's inner needs. "How can I let you know that you still matter to Me? You need to recognize that I continue to be in love with you, especially when I see that you are not at your best." If God's character is guided by such a mind-set, it would be ill-advised for humans to treat one another with anything less.

God's Comfort

Think about the mind-set of the landowner at the end of the day, as he was preparing to pay wages to the laborers. Surely he realized that the workers hired near the end had been struggling with a sense of pessimism since it seemed obvious to them that they would lose their opportunity to go home with some money jingling in their pockets. They had been hired, so that was an encouragement; but they still faced the prospect of collecting little pay. Along with his compassion, the landowner then decided to use this circumstance as a time to send an additional message: "Not only do I care for you, but I want you to feel comforted by the fact that there is someone in your world who will still treat you as a whole person. I want you to see yourself as someone who is to be highly regarded."

Individuals going through the divorce process commonly wonder, "Does this mean that I will now be labeled as a washed-out has-been?" Knowing that many people are more comfortable with those who portray the ideal image of a happily married family person, divorcees might feel ill at ease as the reality settles in that they are not always as welcome in all social circles as they once were. If ever there is a time when comfort is needed, it is during the transition from married to single.

In the Christian world, however, many believers feel increased discomfort when face to face with their divorced brethren. Divorce does not fit neatly into the way things are supposed to be, so it is tempting to shun such untidiness and stick with people who *do* fit the prescribed mold. As they distance themselves from divorcees, they insinuate, "I'm more concerned with my own comfort than I am with extending comfort to you."

Many Christians find it confusing that divorcees can still be deeply committed to Christ even though they have experienced flaws or failure in their lives. The notion of Christians failing somehow seems inconsistent with the truth that the Holy Spirit resides within. They lose sight of the fact that God is not at all shocked that Christians still prove capable of imperfection. Despite the guidance of the Holy Spirit, there can still be problems and failures.

It's also true that a divorced Christian represents a painful reminder that *all* Christians are vulnerable to marital problems. No one is so pure as to say accurately, "That could never happen in my life." To offer comfort to divorcees, there needs to be some amount of identification with those persons' plight. A comforter is likely to think, "I can imagine the hurt you must be going through because I know what I would feel like if the same happened to me." Such empathy causes comforters to momentarily step outside their pleasant surroundings, long enough to consider on a personal level what divorce must be like. This quality can be frightening.

One man candidly told me, "I don't spend time with people who have lost in life because I prefer to think of myself as a winner." Presumably, merely associating with a "loser" would be too close a reminder that he could be similarly vulnerable.

As the Great Comforter, thankfully, God chooses to enter into the hurt of the one who has not had the fullest measure of success, and He emphasizes: "I am with you. Keep on your path and know that I will never leave your side." The apostle Paul chastises Christians who played games of one-upmanship by instructing: "Let no man deceive himself. If any man among you thinks he is wise in this age, let him become foolish that he may become wise" (I Corinthians 3:18). This verse was written in response to criticism from some Christians who believed that Paul did not sufficiently meet their standards as a spokesman for Christ. In verses to follow, he explained that an attitude of arrogance did not draw people to God's heart as did the experience of weakness, being slandered, and being considered "scum" and "dregs" (I Corinthians 4:13). Oddly, Christian growth is found in direct proportion to the willingness to identify with the helplessness that is a by-product of living in a sin-stained world.

Most Christian divorcees can certainly state that they identify with feelings of helplessness. If they allow it, they can also be positioned to receive *all the more* the comfort that comes from knowing that God especially delights in giving comfort where it seems least deserved. Would that all Christians identified with this element of His character.

God's Generosity

In the parable of the vineyard owner and the laborers, the Lord was trying to teach His listeners a different attitude. Rather than being envious of the late workers' good fortune, it would have been desirable for the daylong workers to rejoice with their companions over the generosity shown by the landowner. Similarly, as today's dedicated Christians see how God can bless those who have not produced the same fruit with their lives, it would be better that they rejoice alongside them because of God's gift of grace. By nature, God is exceedingly generous with His benevolence. Let's keep in mind that no humans remotely approach the position of being worthy to receive God's blessings. We are all sinners under the sentence of death. Yet because God is a relationship-loving God, He receives the work of Christ's atonement on our behalf and chooses to give us the blessings that coincide with it.

It is preposterous for one group of redeemed Christians to receive the goodness of God's blessing and then immediately point to another group of Christians to accuse them of being unfit to receive the same. Say a wealthy benefactor takes a beggar off the street, cleans him up, and feeds him a fine meal. Then immediately the benefactor goes back to the street and brings in a second beggar for the same treatment. Suppose, then, the first beggar complains, "You can't be just as nice to him as you were to me because he smells much worse than I ever did!" Such a scene is absurd because the first beggar has absolutely no right to complain about how the benefactor chooses to love people. Christians who declare that divorcees have no business living with the fullness of God's generous blessings have forgotten that they too were just as desperately in need of the gift of salvation. The gift given to them out of the generosity of God's heart is misinterpreted as a right based on merit. As a result, the generosity of God is distorted when the "better" Christians insist that the "lesser" Christians have lost access to God's beneficence.

Speaking with Christians about extending grace to divorcees, I often hear the protest, "Being too lenient toward people who divorce shows that your convictions are watered down." I explain that I continue to hold a deep regard for godly standards, though I have an even higher regard for grace. Consistently I hear a rebuttal like this: "Yeah, that's fine, but I think the Christian community needs to be bold in proclaiming God's will for marriage." My generous spirit can be misconstrued as unwillingness to be true to the evangelistic cause.

Generosity indicates that the one giving the gift recognizes that his own needs are adequately addressed, freeing him to give from a position of excess. Certainly God, being self-sufficient, has much excess to draw upon, the result being His abundant graciousness toward each sinner who calls on Him. Christians not displaying the same generous spirit toward each other sadly reveal a lack of appreciation for the abundance they have received from a forgiving, merciful God. Emotional stinginess instead reveals that there is minimal appreciation of the richness that exists by virtue of being a child of God.

Once Dennis began functioning in his leadership role at his church, he felt a resurgence of God's power in his life. He explained:

"In my past, I've always been picked to be a leader because I have had a history of being a producer, a doer. Quietly, I was pleased with myself as I reasoned that I deserved to be placed in positions that were based on my merit. Now, though, my whole attitude toward my Christian walk is different. I see myself as one who has failed. I guess you could say I'm a loser. Yet, I realize that God is not finished with me. In fact, in many ways I'm beginning a new walk with Him with a fuller understanding of my position in Him. My leadership efforts are no longer accompanied by a sense of deservedness because I don't really see myself as one who deserves much of anything. My leadership efforts are an extension of my joy that God is very generous toward me. If He is so willing to continue giving me the gift of grace, I want the rest of my life to reflect the same willingness to pass along that grace to anyone He puts in my path."

Prior to becoming a divorcee, Dennis assumed that God's love was certainly something to be thankful for. After divorce, he realized it was something that should never be taken for granted. He treasured it so much that he could only do one thing with it: give it away in large doses.

God Is Concerned with Our Spirit

Cynthia sat in my counseling office, crying as she spoke with me about her disillusionment in the aftermath of a conversation she'd had with a member of her church. "He had gotten the word that I was separated from my husband and that I was the one who filed the divorce papers," she told me. "He called me on the phone, and from the very beginning of our conversation I knew he was on a mission to determine if I was guilty of wrongdoing. There was no love in his voice, no concern about my needs, no real desire to know *me*. He was like a police detective who was strictly out to get the facts."

"So how did the conversation play out?"

"Well, once he acknowledged that he knew my husband and I were separated, he asked me to explain why this was happening. I don't really know this man very well, and I didn't like his demeanor;

so I told him we had long-standing problems that had reached a point of impasse, and we were not able to see eye to eye. Immediately, he let me know he needed more information than I was giving, so eventually I told him about my husband's temper tantrums and his temper with our sons. My oldest son is very talented musically, which displeases my husband because he's an old-time jock. Recently, he started calling our son a 'pussy,' saying he'd turn into a 'queer' if he kept up with his sissy priorities."

"You told all this to the member from the church?"

"Yes, but I was reluctant because I just don't want to get drawn into a war of accusations. I told him that the tirades at home occurred a minimum of once a week, and often several times a week. My boys are in their teens now, but they're afraid of their dad because he has been physical several times, breaking dishes and spanking too severely. They've been begging me for a long time to leave him because he's so mean; so, I finally did what I should have done a long time ago when I filed papers."

"So how did the church member respond to your story?"

Cynthia heaved a great sigh through the tears. "The only thing he cared about was the question of adultery. When I told him that was not the issue, he said I'd have to go with him to counseling and stick it out. I tried to explain that we'd had lots of counseling, and nothing would ever change; but he stuck to his insistence and said I would be outside the blessings of God if I followed through with a divorce." Then, shaking her head, she said, "Not once did he ever ask me how I was doing inwardly. He was truly unconcerned with my heart!"

I hear such stories frequently in my counseling office, and it breaks my heart every time. Sometimes people who represent God regrettably bypass the most important elements of relating as they pursue the cold, hard facts. They forget that this is a real person in front of them, with real hurts and emotional needs. If the hurting person's spirit is overlooked, the repercussions can be quite damaging.

Imagine how the landowner came to the conclusion that he should pay the late workers a full day's wage. Though he could have paid solely for the amount of work they had done, he looked beyond the measurable and saw into the souls of those workers. These were people in need, who had been willing to work even though they were previously passed over. Knowing how they would be uplifted on the personal level, he chose to go beyond the call of duty and minister to their sagging spirits with his financial remuneration.

God sees His beloved ones lagging behind in their duties, and He examines them from the inner perspective. "What needs are lacking in you at this time? In what ways do you need to be loved?" He wants each of His followers to rest in the joy that comes from knowing they will be comforted, even if it seems they will not receive comfort.

Ephesians 4:17–24 is a passage that instructs the church (believers) to refrain from futile patterns of life, but to be wholly committed to living in righteousness and holiness. It instructs that we are to refrain from sensuality and every form of impurity. It is one of the many reminders in scripture that God calls us to high standards of morality and responsibility. Unquestionably, Christians are to aim for the highest standards of goodness in every aspect of their lives.

Just prior to this instruction, Ephesians 4:15 says, "Speaking truth in love, we are to grow up in all aspects into Him." Too many Christians pick up on the idea of speaking truth, but they do not follow through with the fact that it is to be done in love. They also miss the message that spiritual growth is a process. Some may say they are speaking truth in love, but there is little evidence that this is the case. Their demeanor is critical and their actions rejecting. Once again the fallen soldier is wounded.

God wants us to know His truth, but not at the expense of losing all sense of His love. When people like Cynthia or Dennis are told they have done a poor job living up to the fullness of God's truth, they are hurt by the negativity of the message; they lose the motivation to fellowship with Christians who would potentially be a healing presence.

Divorce is not pleasant, nor is it desirable. Christians finding themselves in this unwanted situation need people like the landowner who will look beyond mere data and peer into their hearts.

Most Christian divorcees are fully aware of the fact that God does not favor divorce. They are struggling between this truth and the truth that they have been living in a distasteful set of circumstances. If friends and associates are ever going to make progress in the effort to win the hearts of these disenfranchised people, it will happen only after it becomes clear that God's love is an ever-present ingredient.

The subject of divorce is complex and difficult; each divorce has its own sad story. The characters in each story are dear children for whom Christ died. Even as we uphold standards of marital commitment, let us never forget that none of us in the body of Christ are without the need for His grace. Like Jesus, let us find the lost sheep and lovingly bring them back to a place of nurturing.

The Author

Les Carter is the senior psychotherapist at the Minirth Clinic in Richardson, Texas, where he has maintained a private counseling practice since 1980. He is a nationally recognized expert on topics including conflict resolution, emotions and spirituality, and marriage and family relationships. He is the author of twenty books, including *The Anger Trap*, *The Anger Workbook for Christian Parents* (both published by Jossey-Bass), *The Anger Workbook*, *People Pleasers*, and *The Freedom from Depression Workbook*. He can be reached at www.drlescarter.com.

The Anger Trap:
*Free Yourself from the Frustrations
That Sabotage Your Life*

Dr. Les Carter

Hardcover
ISBN: 0-7879-6879-X

"*The Anger Trap* is a masterfully written book, offering penetrating insights into the factors that can imprison individuals in unwanted patterns of frustration. With his well-developed insights and using case examples, Les Carter carefully explains how you can change your thinking, your communication, and your behavior as you release yourself from the ravages of anger gone bad."
—from the Foreword by Frank Minirth, M.D.

"Les Carter has assimilated his years of experience counseling people trapped by anger into a book that I believe will prove helpful to many readers. *The Anger Trap* offers fresh information and understanding that can lead to recovery and reconciliation."
—Zig Ziglar, author and motivational speaker

"The best book on anger out there. Five stars!"
—Dr. Tim Clinton, president, American Association of Christian Counselors

Dr. Les Carter—a nationally recognized expert on the topics of conflict resolution, emotions, and spirituality and coauthor of the best-selling *The Anger Workbook*—has written this practical book that strips away common myths and misconceptions to show viable ways to overcome unhealthy anger and improve relationships. With gentle spiritual wisdom and solid psychological research, Dr. Carter guides you to creating a better, happier life for yourself, your family, and your coworkers.

[Price subject to change]

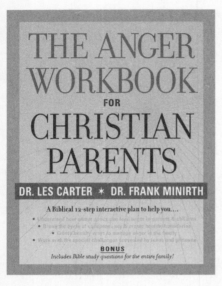

The Anger Workbook for Christian Parents

Dr. Les Carter
and Dr. Frank Minirth

Paperback
ISBN: 0-7879-6903-6

In this practical book, anger experts Dr. Les Carter and Dr. Frank Minirth coauthors of the best-selling book *The Anger Workbook* show families how to understand and manage anger in order to create harmony at home. Blending biblical wisdom and psychological research, they show how to distinguish between healthy and unhealthy anger and offer proven techniques for dealing with the root causes of anger. Full of real-life examples, checklists, evaluation tools, and study questions, this is a "must have" book for those involved with today's youth.

Dr. Les Carter is a nationally known psychotherapist at the Minirth Clinic in Richardson, Texas, where he has practiced since 1980.

Dr. Frank Minirth is president of the Minirth Clinic, which he founded in 1975.

[Price subject to change]

Frank Minirth, M.D.
Don Hawkins, D.MIN.
Roy Vogel, Ph.D.

Just
Like Us

15 Biblical Stories with

Take-Away Messages

You Can Use in Your Life

Just Like Us:

*15 Biblical Stories with
Take-Away Messages You
Can Use in Your Life*

Frank Minirth, M.D.
Don Hawkins, D.Min.
Roy Vogel, Ph.D.

Cloth
ISBN: 0-7879-6904-4

"This is the best series of biographical studies of Bible characters I
have seen. The balance of solid
biblical truth and sound psychological insight is just right. It's a
valuable manual for personal study and improvement as well as a gold
mine for teachers and preachers of the Bible."

—Warren W. Wiersbe, author and conference speaker

"The Bible is living history focused on ordinary personalities. Though some
were anointed by God with 'beyond the norm' supernatural gifts and
abilities, their humanness with all its weaknesses remains intact. This book
helps us focus on these ordinary personalities and the spiritual lessons we
can learn; particularly from this 'humanness' that is 24/7 reality for all of us.
I recommend it highly."

—Dr. Gene A. Getz, pastor emeritus, Fellowship Bible Church North,
and director, Center for Church Renewal, Plano, Texas

"If you've ever felt a disconnect with all those Bible heroes, *Just Like Us*
is for you. The authors turn them into your friends and neighbors. You'll
see their fears and foibles are as common as your own and learn how to
connect with God's power as they did."

—Dr. Woodrow Kroll, president, *Back to the Bible*

Dr. Frank Minirth is president of the Minirth Clinic in Richardson, Texas,
which he founded in 1975. He has authored or coauthored fifty books,

including the best-selling *Happiness Is a Choice*, *Love Is a Choice*, and *Love Hunger*. He is featured on Life Perspective with Don Hawkins, a national program on 55 radio stations, and on American Family Radio, another national program with two-minute spots on 200 radio stations in America. He writes short digests for the Web site, www.minirthclinic.com.

Don Hawkins, formerly the cohost and producer of the *Back to the Bible* radio program, which is on more than six hundred stations worldwide, and host of the live nationwide call-in program *Life Perspectives*, serves as the president of Southeastern Bible College in Birmingham, Alabama.

Roy Vogel is a psychologist and board-certified pharmacologist based in New Jersey. He is founder of Advent Counseling Centers and host of the New Jersey radio program *Lyrics to Live By*.